LOCOMOTIVES
in detail

MAUNSELL 4-6-0 | **4** | **KING ARTHUR CLASS**

LOCOMOTIVES

in detail

4

MAUNSELL 4-6-0   **KING ARTHUR CLASS**

PETER SWIFT

Ian Allan
PUBLISHING

In compiling this book, I am heavily indebted to the many writers who have described the Maunsell 'King Arthur' class 4-6-0s in the past. Most of the story is already in print, and only needed putting into the order required for this book. The most useful of these books are listed in the bibliography, in the order of publication.

For additional information, I am indebted to Ann Bradley, widow of the late Don Bradley, who donated Don's research material to the care of the South Western Circle, and to Philip Atkins and his staff at the National Railway Museum, who made available the engine and boiler record cards. I am also indebted to Philip for pointing out the connection between the Indian BESA standard 4-6-0s, T.S. Finlayson and the Urie 4-6-0s of the LSWR.

For the provision of photographs, I am indebted to all those photographers whose material has found its way into my own collection over many years, in many cases with no record of the source. Peter Waller of the Ian Allan organisation allowed me access to the Ian Allan photographic archive. Richard Casserley has provided prints from the vast H. C. Casserley negative archive and Mike King has supplied prints from the Ted West collection, which he holds on behalf of the South Western Circle. Rod Blencowe has also supplied prints to fill some of the gaps in the pictorial story of the 'King Arthurs'.

The late George Woodward kept a week by week record of everything which came into Eastleigh Works from 1926 to the 1960s. Without his notes, all subsequent writers would have been left guessing on many aspects of what happened, particularly regarding liveries, that most contentious of issues with modellers. I owe an enormous debt of gratitude to Eric Youldon of Exeter, who was a close observer of 'King Arthurs' over many years and who has gone through my drafts and added amendments, additions and corrections which had never occurred to me before. Eric also put me in touch with John Harvey, who sorted out some of the tender exchanges, and Barry Fletcher, who provided the information on the colour of the 'King Arthur' nameplates at different periods.

This book is dedicated to all those who have worked at Eastleigh locomotive works under its successive ownership by the London & South Western Railway, Southern Railway, British Railways, British Rail Engineering Ltd and Alstom. The closure of the works, after 96 years of building and overhauling steam locomotives and, latterly, overhauling diesel and electric stock, was announced at the time this book was being written.

Peter Swift, Spondon, Derby, June 2005

Bibliography
S. C. Townroe. *King Arthurs and Lord Nelsons of the SR*. Ian Allan 1949.
H. Holcroft. *Locomotive Adventure Volume 1*. Ian Allan 1962.
H. Holcroft. *Locomotive Adventure Volume 2*. Ian Allan 1965.
D. L. Bradley. *Locomotives of the L&SWR Part 2*. RCTS 1967.
L. Tavender. *Livery Register No. 3 LSWR and Southern*. HMRS 1970
S. C. Townroe. *The Arthurs, Nelsons and Schools of the Southern*. Ian Allan 1973
O. S. Nock. *The Southern King Arthur Family*. David & Charles 1976.
D. L. Bradley. *Locomotive History of the SE&CR*. RCTS 1980.
S. C. Townroe. *Arthurs, Nelsons & Schools at Work*. Ian Allan 1982.
B. Haresnape. *Railway Liveries - Southern Railway*. Ian Allan 1982.
D. L. Bradley. *LSWR Locomotives - The Urie Classes*. Wild Swan 1987.
P. Atkins. *The James Clayton Influence*. Railways S East 1988/9.
H. Hughes. *Indian Locomotives Part 1 Broad Gauge 1851-1940*. Continental Railway Circle 1990
P. Atkins. *Private Locomotive Builders and the Indian Connection*. Bedside Backtrack. Atlantic Publishing 1993.
J. E. Chacksfield. *Richard Maunsell An Engineering Biography*. Oakwood 1998.

Series Created & Edited by Jasper Spencer-Smith.
Design and artwork: Nigel Pell.
Produced by JSS Publishing Limited, P.O. Box 6031, Bournemouth, Dorset, England.

Title spread: 'Scotchman' No 30787 *Sir Menadeuke* and No 30784 *Sir Nerovens* at Eastleigh, April 1957. (CR)

First published 2005

ISBN (10) 0711030863
ISBN (13) 978 0 7110 3086 2

Published by Ian Allan Publishing

an imprint of Ian Allan Publishing Ltd, Hersham, Surrey KT12 4RG.
Printed in England by Ian Allan Printing Ltd, Hersham, Surrey KT12 4RG.

Code: 0509/B2

Visit the Ian Allan Publishing website at www.ianallanpublishing.com

Photograph Credits
Colour-Rail (CR) and photographers
A. E. R. Cope (EC); Ian Davidson (ID);
G. H. Hunt (GHH); A. A. Jarvis (AAJ);
J. Kinnison (JK); W. Potter (WP); S. C. Townroe (ST).
Authors Collection (AC).
Ian Allan Library (IA) and photographers
B. W. Anwell (BWA); Colin Boocock (CB);
Rev. A. C. Cawston (ACC); R. F. Dearden (RFD);
M. W. Earley (MWE); L. Elsey (LE); C. J. Grose (CJG);
G. F. Heiron (GFH); G. J. Jefferson (GJJ); F. F. Moss (FFM);
K. R. Nunn (KRN); R. C. Riley (RCR); G. Rixon (GR);
J. Scrace (JS); G. Wheeler (GW); P. Ransome Wallis (PRW);
Others:
D. L. Bradley (DLB); R. K. Blencoe/Transport Treasury (RKB); Rev. A. C. Cawston/R. K. Blencoe (AC/AKB); H. C. Casserley (HCC); M. J. Fox (MJF);
Dr. Richard Green (RG); W. Gilburt (WG);
N. Pomfret Collection (NP); W. J. Reynolds (WJR);
Stephenson Locomotive Society (SLS);
A. E. West/South Western Circle (AEW/SWC).

INTRODUCTION

The Maunsell 'King Arthur' class locomotives of the
Southern Railway were developed from an existing
London & South Western Railway type by the design team
of the former South Eastern & Chatham Railway.

The prime aim of this series of books is to provide modellers with information on the appearance of the locomotives at each period of their history. To this end, photographs of as many of the variants as possible, covering as many of the livery variants as possible, are included, together with accurate scale drawings. Within the Maunsell 'King Arthur' class of the Southern Railway (SR), there were four basic varieties of locomotive, the first of which was already in existence before the SR was formed, and before Maunsell and his team had any influence on the design. In order to help modellers to run appropriate locomotives on layouts set in defined locations, information is given on where the different varieties of 'King Arthur' operated, and the captions of some photographs make reference to train formations, an aspect ignored on many, otherwise excellent, model railway layouts. Apart from where shortcomings led to modifications to the appearance of the locomotives, little reference is made to performance on the line.

Some locomotive designs were dominated by one man, a classic example being the Southern Railway 'Pacifics' of that 'wayward' genius Oliver Bulleid. Others were the production of a team, such as the locomotives designed and built at Swindon between 1920 and 1950, after G.J. Churchward had shown them how it should be achieved. The 'King Arthurs' were produced by two different teams, which did not always concur. The Eastleigh team under Robert Urie provided their robust dependability and Maunsell's team added the sparkle. Before describing the 'King Arthur' class, it is necessary to introduce the teams and give a brief description of what they had produced before the 'King Arthurs' came onto the scene.

THE EASTLEIGH TEAM

In November 1912, Dugald Drummond, Chief Mechanical Engineer of the London & South Western Railway (LSWR), died and the company's board of directors appointed Robert Urie, the Manager of the LSWR's Eastleigh Works, to succeed him. Drummond had a reputation for irascibility, but Robert Urie was one of a number of Scottish locomotive men who could see the leadership behind the bark and had followed Drummond south, when he moved to the LSWR in 1895. Two others were Drummond's chief draughtsman J.A. Hunter and Tom Finlayson, who was appointed chief draughtsman at Eastleigh by Robert Urie. Finlayson had previously worked with the North British Locomotive Company in Glasgow, and had been involved in the design of the British Engineering Standards Association's (BESA) standard 4-6-0s for the railways of India.

Above:
Which way from here? LSWR No 459 was the last of Drummond's four-cylinder 4-6-0s to be built in July 1912. The Class T14 had four cylinders in line below the smokebox but with a better grate and ashpan, could have been good locomotives. One forward looking feature was that just two sets of outside Walschaerts valve gear, with the inside valves worked by rocking levers from the outside valve rods, were fitted. (AC)

Left:
North British Locomotive Co-built 'Scotchman' No 766 *Sir Geraint* at Nine Elms, April 1947, is painted in 1946-style Malachite Green livery, with green smoke deflectors and wheels. (CR/HJ)

Right:
The precursor to the 'King Arthur' class, the Robert Urie-designed 'H15' class 4-6-0. No 483 is photographed at Eastleigh when new in 1914, with a Schmidt-type superheater. The arrangement of the valve gear is identical to that on the BESA 4-6-0. Piston tailrods were fitted initially. (AC)

Right:
The Finlayson input. No 411 *Hero,* a BESA standard 4-6-0 of the Great Indian Peninsular Railway, was actually built by the Vulcan Foundry in 1921 but apart from the feedwater heater, top feed and oil tank, is virtually identical to the locomotives built by the North British Locomotive Company (NBL) for the Indian railways from 1910. One feature which Finlayson did not copy on LSWR locomotives was the Belpaire firebox . (IA)

Dugald Drummond had been one of the leading locomotive designers of the late 1800s, with a series of excellent inside cylinder 4-4-0 locomotives built between 1876 and 1912 for the North British Railway, Caledonian Railway and London & South Western Railway. However, he had overreached his own skills with a series of four-cylinder 4-6-0s, built for the LSWR between 1905 and 1912. Drummond's later locomotives were provided with cross water tubes in the firebox and feedwater heaters. These provided improved steam raising capacity and a reduction in coal consumption, but at the expense of reliability and maintenance costs. As Works Manager, Urie had seen the problems with the Drummond locomotives but also realised that the inside cylinder 4-4-0 type had reached the limit of development.

The Urie locomotives for the LSWR were all massively built, with two outside cylinders surmounted by piston valves operated by Walschaerts valve gear. All except two, which were quickly brought into line, were provided with superheaters. Walschaerts valve gear was not new, Egide Walschaerts, head of traction of the Belgian State Railways at Brussels South, had patented it in 1848 and it was well established in Continental Europe by the 1880s. However, British railway engineers were very slow to adopt the valve gear, tending to remain with Stephenson's link inside motion even on locomotives with outside cylinders. Daily tasks, such as inspection or lubrication of the valve gear had to be carried out from a pit under the locomotive, or by peering under the boiler from the running plate. With Walschaerts gear, these jobs, and maintenance of the gear, could be carried out by a man standing

Left:
'H15' class No 489, passing Earlsfield on an up semi-fast from Bournemouth. All three constituents of the Southern Railway used fixed formation trainsets for the majority of services. This train contains a '4½ set' of four non-corridor coaches and a six-wheeled van, augmented by a third class coach on the front and with a tail load of vans. The very new insulators of the third rail on the up local line, suggest that the date is 1914. (IA)

Left:
SE&CR Maunsell 'N' class No 820, built at Ashford, 1922, in the SE&CR's wartime grey livery with company ownership denoted by a small plate on the cabside. The serif-style buffer beam numerals and the large number on the tender were perpetuated on the Southern. The smokebox door and cab roof was used on the 'Scotchmen'. The small tender was fitted on the second series Eastleigh 'Arthurs'. Unlike the LSWR, the SE&CR used conventional lamp irons. (AC)

beside the locomotive. British locomotive builders had used outside Walschaerts gear for export locomotives for some years, the BESA standard 4-6-0s for India (with which Tom Finlayson would have been familiar) had Walschaerts gear from 1908. Apart from some oddities, such as a Fairlie articulated 0-4-4T which the Swindon, Marlborough & Andover Railway obtained in 1877, the regular use of Walschaerts gear on British railways started with the steam railcar craze of the 1900s. The first two-cylinder main line locomotives with outside Walschaerts gear to be built for a British railway were Sir Nigel Gresley's 2-6-0 and 2-8-0 classes, constructed at Doncaster for the Great Northern Railway in 1911.

Drummond had used Walschaerts gear on the outside cylinders of his 4-6-0s, in conjunction with Stephenson's gear for the inside cylinders, on the earlier locomotives. His 'T14' class of 1911

used two sets of Walschaerts gear for the outside cylinders, with the valves of the inside cylinders worked by rocking levers from the outside valve spindles. At the time of Drummond's death, the Eastleigh drawing office was working on the design of a four-cylinder 0-8-0 (Order No H15) and a mixed traffic 4-6-0 (Order No K15). Five of each had been ordered. Urie cancelled work on these, and re-used the order numbers for 10 of his own design of mixed traffic 4-6-0, classified 'H15' on the Southern. When No 486 emerged from Eastleigh Works at the end of 1913, the valve gear was probably seen by the Eastleigh design staff merely as the logical application of their existing practice to a two-cylinder locomotive. However No 486 also happened to be the first 4-6-0 with two simple outside cylinders and Walschaerts valve gear to run on a British railway, foreshadowing the 'Black 5', 'B1' and BR Standard Class 4 and 5

Top:
'H15' class No 486, as built in 1914 with a Robinson-type superheater. When new, the 'H15s' carried the Drummond LSWR passenger livery, with purple brown edging and double lining. The artist has missed the lined panel on the tender bogie frames. (AC)

which hauled the majority of passenger and fast freight traffic on Britain's railways during the final years of steam traction. Despite its modern appearance, there were features of the design which were not in line with current developments elsewhere. The valve travel was only $5^{1}/_{8}$in (13.02cm) and the balancing of the heavy reciprocating masses, designed to minimise fore and aft surging of the locomotive, resulted in the driving axle producing a very heavy hammer blow effect on the track.

Although looking very different at first sight from any of Drummond's locomotives, there was still a lot of Drummond influence in the design, to which were added features from the Indian standard 4-6-0s, such as the cylinder and valve gear arrangement and the narrowing of the frames in front of the coupled wheels, allowing larger cylinders to fit within the loading gauge. The large parallel boiler was dimensionally the same as those

used on Drummond's earliest 4-6-0s of 1905/7 and the proposed 0-8-0 of 1912, but the firebox of the Urie boilers was 6in (15.24cm) shorter and with a sloping grate for easier firing. The chimney, dome and cased direct loading safety valves were as on the Drummond 4-6-0s, as was the smokebox door, but with a centre dart closure reinforced by four dogs at the bottom where distortion was most likely due to ash accumulation. Urie fitted firetube superheaters, which Drummond had never used although he had put smokebox superheaters in a few locomotives.

Of the 10 'H15s', four were fitted with a Schmidt-type superheater, four with a Robinson-type superheater and two were initially without superheaters. With the benefits of superheating proven Urie designed his own version, referred to as the Eastleigh superheater, which was later fitted to all 10 locomotives. The cab, with deep side cut outs and arched roof with pronounced eaves, was

also a Drummond design but the pear-shaped cab spectacles (front windows) were new, and were to be a characteristic feature of all the Urie/Maunsell two-cylinder 4-6-0s. The high running plate, leaving the whole of the cylinders and valve gear visible, was new. On the 'H15s', the running plate dropped down behind the cylinders, resulting in a long, shallow, splasher being fitted over the driving wheels.

Like the locomotive, the tender looked new, but was actually very similar to the large bogie tenders built by Drummond for his 'T14' class 4-6-0s in 1912. The Urie tender looked different, because it had outside framed bogies and plates for retaining the coal on the tender in place of the open rails on the Drummond pattern. The tenders for the 'H15' class were smaller than those on the 'T14s', carrying 5,200 gallons (23,639 litres) of water, compared with the 5,800-gallon (26,367-litre) 'T14' tenders. The two water fillers,

either side at the rear of the tender, and the arrangement of the handbrake, shovelling plate, toolboxes and sandboxes at the front of the tender were the same.

Having designed the mixed traffic 4-6-0 'H15' class in 1914, Urie had planned express passenger and goods versions and, in January 1916, the locomotive committee authorised 10 express and five goods locomotives. Due to the World War 1, Government authority was required to build them which was not received until mid-1918. The first 10 of what later became the 'King Arthur' class were completed at Eastleigh in 1919 to Order Nos N15 and P15. The 'N15' classification was given to the whole class, including the Maunsell derivatives in Southern Railway days. The design followed that of the 'H15', but with 6ft 7in (200.66cm) driving wheels, longer wheelbase, larger cylinders and a taper boiler. The locomotives were fitted with

stovepipe chimneys, and the running plate was level from the cylinders to the cab.

The first 10 express 4-6-0s were followed by 20 for express freight traffic, known as Class S15, four 4-8-0Ts ('G16') and five 4-6-2Ts ('H16'). These were built as part of a major investment by the LSWR in its freight facilities, including the construction of a new marshalling yard at Feltham in west London. Finally, a further 10 express 4-6-0s were ordered, the last three of which were not completed at the end of 1922. To complete this survey of Urie's contribution to Southern motive power the six earliest and worst of Drummond's 4-6-0s were rebuilt as 'H15s', retaining the boilers and tenders of the originals. Maunsell authorised the building of 10 more 'H15s' in 1924, but with the taper boiler and 5,000-gallon (22,730-litre) tender of the 'N15' and 'S15' classes.

THE MAUNSELL TEAM

In 1913, locomotive affairs on the railways run by the South Eastern & Chatham Railway (SE&CR) joint managing committee were in a mess. Due to a combination of board parsimony and mismanagement the closure of the old London, Chatham & Dover Railway works at Longhedge (Battersea) London and transfer of all work to the SE&CR's works at Ashford in Kent had resulted in a severe shortage of usable locomotives at a time of increasing traffic. The locomotive carriage and wagon superintendent, H.S. Wainwright, accepted the blame and retired in November 1913 at the early age of 49. In searching for a successor, the SE&CR board's

requirement was primarily for an able manager, and found one in the person of Richard Edward Lloyd Maunsell, locomotive superintendent of the Great Southern & Western Railway (GS&WR) in Ireland. Maunsell was appointed as Chief Mechanical Engineer.

Maunsell was born in 1868, to a County Dublin family of English extraction. He studied law at Trinity College, Dublin and concurrently became a pupil to H.A. Ivatt, the locomotive superintendent of the GS&WR at Inchicore (Dublin). Having gained further experience on the Lancashire & Yorkshire Railway and the East Indian Railway, he returned to the GS&WR in 1896 as assistant locomotive engineer and works manager under the newly appointed locomotive superintendent, Robert Coey. When Coey retired in 1911, Maunsell was appointed to the top job at Inchicore. The only new locomotives built at Inchicore during his superintendence were eight 0-6-0s and a single large 4-4-0, both of which were developments of designs prepared under Coey's chief draughtsman, Ernest Joynt.

On arrival at the Ashford Works in December 1913, Maunsell's first priority was to sort out the mess in the works (which he did) but that is beyond the scope of this book. That he was not fully conversant with the finer points of locomotive design is shown by the curious case of the 'L' class. When Maunsell arrived, the drawings had been prepared for the new 'L' class 4-4-0 passenger locomotive, nominally a Wainwright design but actually designed under the control of Wainwright's chief draughtsman, Robert Surtees. Being unsure of the standard of design work at Ashford, Maunsell sent

Left:
'H15' class No 475 at Nine Elms in 1924. Although built in Southern Railway days, the only Maunsell feature of the design was the crosshead-driven vacuum pump mounted on the left-hand lower slidebar. All were initially painted in late LSWR passenger green livery, but with Southern-style lettering and no cabside numberplate. Nine were built with the Eastleigh-type superheater but No 524 had a Maunsell-type superheater. (AC)

copies of the drawings to Joynt at Inchicore. Joynt recommended some changes, including a reduction to the valve travel. At the time some locomotive engineers, in particular G.J. Churchward of the Great Western Railway (GWR), were obtaining freer running and reduced fuel consumption by the use of longer valve travel. Others clearly, including Joynt, were afraid that this would lead to greater wear of the valves. They were partially right, but the gain in economy far outweighed the extra wear, particularly after valves and their lubrication had been developed to cope with the greater valve speeds. Maunsell accepted Joynt's recommendation, with the result that the 'L' class, although good haulers, were not fast running locomotives.

Maunsell may not have been able personally to design a good locomotive, but he knew what he wanted, and set about building up a team that could. When Surtees retired he was replaced by James Clayton, the assistant chief draughtsman on the Midland Railway at Derby. Clayton had a wide experience of innovative engineering. After training with Beyer Peacock and as a draughtsman at Ashford he worked in the newly developing motor industry before being taken into the personal employment of Cecil Paget. Paget was locomotive works manager at Derby and son of the Midland Railway's chairman, and was building, at his own cost, a 2-6-2 with four double-ended cylinders, sleeve valves and dry-sided firebox - 40 years before Bulleid's Leader class! When Paget's brainchild failed to come up to expectations, Clayton had moved into the drawing office at Derby.

From Churchward's team at Swindon came carriage works manager George Pearson, as Maunsell's assistant chief mechanical engineer and works manager. Harold Holcroft, who had been employed on special projects under Churchward (including producing the outline design for the '43xx' class 2-6-0s) became Maunsell's personal assistant. With Pearson and Holcroft, the techniques which made Churchward's GWR locomotives such a success had been transferred to another British railway for the first time. It was to take another 20 years before all four of the post-Grouping railways were in on the secret.

Maunsell's team quickly produced drawings for a 2-6-0 (Class N) for freight work and a 2-6-4T (Class K) for express passenger work. The 2-6-4T was similar to one designed, but not built, at Derby for the Fenchurch Street to Southend services and the 2-6-0 could almost be described as a cross between Holcroft's '43xx' 2-6-0 for the GWR and Clayton's 2-8-0 designed for the Somerset & Dorset Joint Railway (S&DJR) shortly before he left Derby. Both classes had the taper boiler and long travel piston valves of Swindon practice, but with domes on the boilers and outside Walschaerts valve gear. Superficial details, such as the cab and tender, might have come straight off a Midland Compound. Due to World War 1 restrictions, only a single prototype of each type was built in 1917. Later 15 further 2-6-0s were built between 1920 and 1923, and the numbers of both types were increased in Southern Railway days including 50 from a batch of one hundred 2-6-0s built at The Woolwich Arsenal as a Government initiative, to avoid postwar unemployment.

CHAPTER ONE

THE FOUR SUB-CLASSES

The 74 locomotives of the Southern 'King Arthur' class comprised four sub-classes, built to operate on different sections of the Southern Railway. There was also a small-wheeled freight version.

The first batch of 20 'King Arthurs' were not Maunsell locomotives at all, being built for the London & South Western Railway under the direction of Chief Mechanical Engineer, Robert Urie.

THE URIE ARTHURS

The first 10 of what later became the 'King Arthur' class were completed at Eastleigh, Nos 736 to 740 to Order No 'N15' and Nos 741 to 745 to Order No P15. The 'N15' classification was given to the whole class, as well as the Maunsell derivatives, in Southern Railway days. The 5,000-gallon (22,730-litre) bogie tenders for these locomotives were built to Order Nos O15 and R15. The locomotives entered service between August 1918 and November 1919. The design followed that of the 'H15', but with 6ft 7in (200.66cm) driving wheels, longer wheelbase, larger cylinders and a taper boiler. The locomotives were fitted with stovepipe chimneys, and the running plate was straight from the cylinders to the cab. A single long splasher each side covered the tops of the coupled wheels. The tender was 6in (15.24cm) shallower but 4in (10.16cm) wider than that provided for the 'H15' class of locomotive.

A second batch of "N15's" were authorised, Nos 746 to 750 to Order No L16 and Nos 751 to 755 to Order No N16, with tenders to Order Nos M16 and O16. All entered traffic between June 1922 and March 1923, the last three delivered after the formation of the Southern Railway, were finished in LSWR livery. On the first 10 locomotives, Nos 736 to 745, the slidebars were fluted but on Nos 746 to 755 these were plain. On all the locomotives, the slidebars were the same thickness throughout the length.

When the 'N15' class first entered to traffic, there was still a wartime speed restriction of 60mph (97kph) and the locomotives appeared to be adequate for the requirements. However, when the speed restrictions were lifted and train timings tightened during the summer of 1922, it became apparent that the 'N15' class would not steam properly. In the few months before World War 1, the 'H15s' had shown themselves to be very free steaming - so why not the 'N15'. In an attempt to get the exhaust to rise clear of the boiler, the stovepipe chimney was of a smaller internal diameter than that of the 'H15s' lipped chimney; this was restricting the exhaust. The Urie-type superheater may have been partly to blame; it required more space in the smokebox than the Schmidt or Robinson-type superheater fitted to the 'H15s', or the later Maunsell-type superheater.

Above:
Urie 'N15' class
No 740 *Merlin*, at
Nine Elms when
new. The first 10
Urie 'Arthurs',
Nos 737 to 745, had
fluted slidebars.
Locomotives Nos 746
to 755 were fitted
with plain slide bars.
(AC)

Left:
Urie 'N15' class
No 747 *Elaine*
approaching Esher
on a Bournemouth
express in the early
1920s. (AC)

Although guidelines were available, locomotive 'draughting' was always a bit of a black art. One only has to think of examples of later locomotives, designed by teams with far greater resources than the small Eastleigh design team, which failed to steam properly when new. The LMS 'Jubilees', the GWR '78xx' 'Manors' and the LMS Class 2 all come immediately to mind. It must have been galling for the Eastleigh team to have the weakness of its design exposed, just at the time when Maunsell and his bright young men came onto the scene.

Line tests were carried out on No 742, leading to alterations to the valve settings, provision of a larger diameter lipped chimney and reduction in cylinder diameter to 1ft 9in (53.54cm). These alterations brought considerable improvements and were applied to all the locomotives, although the Urie 'Arthurs' were generally never considered to be as good as those with the Maunsell chimney. The chimney finally adopted was very similar to the Drummond-type on the first batch of 'H15s', the taper boiler keeping it within the lower SR composite loading gauge.

THE EASTLEIGH ARTHURS

At the Grouping, the LSWR still had 15 of the earlier Drummond four-cylinder 4-6-0s in its inventory, although not all were in use. The 'F13'

Above:
Urie 'Arthur' No E755 *The Red Knight*, near Earlsfield on an up Bournemouth express composed of late LSWR 'Ironclad' stock. The stovepipe chimney has a reduced capuchon and there is a louvre in the front of the chimney. Nothing is known of this experiment, which may have been an early smoke deflector trial or may have been a means of creating an upward draught during running when the regulator and blower were closed. (SLS)

Left:
No E752 *Linette* on a Portsmouth express in Clapham cutting circa 1926. The locomotive is in full Southern livery but is otherwise as built. (RG)

series (Nos 330 to 334 of 1905) were rebuilt as 'H15s' in 1924. Also there was a proposal to do the same to the 'G14' and 'P14' series (Nos 453 to 457 of 1908 and Nos 448 to 452 of 1911). The rebuild would have been more expensive than that of the 'F13s', as the 'G14s' and 'P14s' had smaller boilers so new would be required. However, the locomotive running department did not require more mixed traffic 4-6-0s, but there was a need for more express 4-6-0s. Maunsell set Eastleigh drawing office the task of amending the 'N15' design to include cylinders, valve gear and draughting in line with the principles adopted at Ashford. The Urie coned boiler was uprated to work at a pressure of 200 psi (13.6 bar), fitted

with a Maunsell-type superheater and a lipped chimney, shorter than the stovepipe-type to fit the lower loading gauge of the eastern section. Because the locomotives were intended for the western section, the Urie-type cab roof was retained. All were built to Eastleigh Order No B17 (Nos 453 to 457) and Order No C17 (Nos 448 to 452). Apart from the tenders, Eastleigh 'Arthurs' incorporated no fittings from the 'G14' and 'P14' locomotives. No 449, renumbered as E0449, continued to run until October 1927 with the driving axle set to give eight exhaust beats per rotation of the wheels. This arrangement was later adopted for the Maunsell-designed 'Lord Nelson' class 4-6-0s.

There were a number of visible changes from the Urie 'Arthurs'. The high pressure steam pipe from the superheater to the cylinders was routed through the side of the smokebox to the top of the valve chest, the pipe's cladding filling the space between the running plate and the smokebox. The flat cover-plate over the top of the cylinders on Urie locomotives was removed. The Eastleigh 'Arthurs', and the other Maunsell 'King Arthurs', perpetuated the plain slidebars of the second series of Urie 'Arthurs', but there was now a taper at the end away from the cylinder to the outer edge of the slidebars. The other visible change was the provision of a crosshead driven vacuum pump, mounted below the lower left-hand slidebar.

In order to achieve the longer valve travel, the reversing cross shaft was moved forward approximately 1in (2.5cm) and the arm which lifts the radius rod made 1in (2.5cm) longer. The expansion die block was also longer to allow for the increased vertical movement of the end of the radius rod. Otherwise the valve gear remained the same. The Urie 'Arthurs' had followed Drummond's practice in fitting coil springs for the driving axle and leaf springs for the leading and trailing coupled axles. All the Maunsell 'Arthurs' had leaf springs for all three axles.

A minor change was made to the running plate valance. On the Urie 'Arthurs', a small fillet was fitted at both front and rear as a connection to

Above:
No E453 *King Arthur*
as built. The name-
plate does not have
the 'King Arthur Class'
lettering below the
main name. Visible
changes from the Urie
'Arthurs' include a
lipped chimney,
outside high-pressure
steam pipes and the
crosshead-driven
vacuum pump
mounted below the
left-hand lower
slidebar. The Ross Pop
safety valves and the
snifting valves show
that the locomotive
has a 200 psi boiler,
with a Maunsell-type
superheater. (AC)

Left:
The right-hand side of
No E452 *Sir
Meliagrance*.
A vacuum pump is not
fitted on this
side. The plate across
the back of the coal
space is in the usual
position, at the rear
drop of the coal
rails. Whereas that on
the tender of E453
(above) is set further
forward. (AC)

the buffer beam and dragbox. The first series Eastleigh 'Arthurs' had this fillet only at the buffer beam. The final visible change from the Urie 'Arthurs' was, of course, the nameplate. These were straight, except for No E453 *King Arthur*, and had the wording 'King Arthur Class' in small letters below the name. The plates were in a range of standard lengths, depending on the length of the name. They were mounted on the splasher, centred above the driving wheel. The nameplate of No E453 *King Arthur* was initially mounted at half depth on the splasher, but on the other locomotives the plates were mounted with the upper edges flush with the top of the splasher. The plate on No E453 *King Arthur* was later re-located.

THE SCOTCHMEN (OR SCOTCH ARTHURS)

At the Grouping, the standard of the track on the ex-SE&CR main lines precluded the use of heavy locomotives, although something larger than the rebuilt 4-4-0s was badly needed for the Continental services. By 1925 much of the track had been upgraded and 30 more 'King Arthurs' were ordered for use on both the eastern and western sections. All were ordered from the North British Locomotive Company (NBL) of Glasgow, as the workshops of the SR did not have the capacity to build that number of locomotives in the time required.

Above:
No E449 *Sir Torre was* the Southern Railway's exhibit at the Stockton & Darlington Railway centenary parade on 2 July 1925. For the event, a Urie tender was fitted, and retained at least until September 1925. The train consists of a set of the 'Thanet' stock built in 1924 for the Ramsgate and Dover services. (KRN

Centre:
No E450 *Sir Kay* approaching Clapham Junction on a West of England express in the 1920s. The main train consists of LSWR timber-bodied corridor stock with the dining saloon in the centre augmented with three elderly LSWR non-corridor coaches on the front. (AC)

Right:
No E456 *Sir Galahad* on a semi-fast from Salisbury passing through Clapham cutting in the 1920s. (RG)

Above:
No E764 *Sir Gawain* as built. Basically the same as the Eastleigh 'Arthurs', the rounded cab roof and the Urie-pattern tender gave the 'Scotchmen' a more modern appearance. The circular works plate on the smoke-box side indicates that it was built by the North British Locomotive Company. (AC)

Left:
'Scotchman' No E788 *Sir Urre of the Mount* as built. This locomotive was originally to have been named *Sir Beaumains*. It is thought that the nameplates of this locomotive together with those for No E767 *Sir Valance* and No E787 *Sir Menadeuke*, which were also second choice names, were made by the SR as the plates have slight differences from those made by NBL. (AC)

Having been formed out of three railway companies, the Southern had three different loading gauges. Ignoring details of what happened below platform level, these may be summarised as:

Section	Width	Height	Top Radius
Western (LSWR)	9ft 3in (282cm)	13ft 4in (406.4cm)	5ft 6in (167.6cm)
Central (LB&SCR)	9ft 0in (274.3cm)	13ft 6in (411.5cm)	7ft 6in (213.4cm)
Eastern (SE&CR)	9ft 0in (274.3cm)	13ft 1in (398.8cm)	5ft 9in (175.3cm)

The Southern developed a Composite Loading Gauge; effectively that of the eastern section.

The Urie and Eastleigh 'Arthurs' had been built to the LSWR loading gauge and were 9ft 1in (276.9cm) wide over the running plate, but every-thing else was within the 9ft (274.3cm) width limit. The capuchon on the original Urie-type stovepipe chimney was 13ft 2^1/$_2$in (403.2cm) above rail, but the Maunsell-type chimney was only 12ft 11^1/$_2$in (395cm) above rail. As a result ^{1}/$_2$in (1.3cm) was shaved off each side of the running plate, also the cab was redesigned with the sides and roof smoothly merging. The cab roof was extended back over the tender fallplate as on the 2-6-0 'N' class. The pear shape of the cab spectacles was amended with a straight lower edge. The only other difference from the Eastleigh 'Arthurs' was the smokebox door: a Maunsell type with no central dart and six closing dogs.

Twenty locomotives had been ordered from NBL on 17 December 1924 and 10 more on 28 January 1925. The manufacturing resources of Britain's largest locomotive works allowed the 30 'Scotchmen', Nos 763 to 792, to be delivered between May and October 1925. The gap in the number series between the last Urie 'Arthur' (No 755 *The Red Knight*) and the first 'Scotchman' (No 763 *Sir Bors de Ganis*) had been filled by the

Above:
No E775 *Sir Agravaine* in Clapham cutting on an up West of England express in the late 1920s. The main part of the train is now Maunsell corridor stock. An LSWR steel-panelled brake composite of 1918 and a third have probably come from one of the east Devon branches. (RG)

Right:
No E764 *Sir Gawain* departs Victoria on a boat train in the 1920s, whilst another 'Scotchman' waits on the left. Both trains consist of the carriages built specifically for the Continental boat train services between 1921 and 1927. To the right is one of 10 ex-LSWR Drummond 'L12' class 4-4-0s, which were transferred to the eastern section in 1925. The American-style three position upper-quadrant signals were installed in 1919. (AC)

Above:
No E766 *Sir Geraint* heading the 'Dover Pullman Continental Express', which became the 'Golden Arrow' in 1929. One of the Pullman cars initially allocated to SE&CR services is coupled to K-type cars of the 1920s. (RG)

Left:
A classic railway image, C.E.Brown's photograph of his son talking to the driver at Waterloo is best known as the Southern's 'Summer Comes Soonest in the South' poster. The incomplete retouching shows that No 750 *Morgan le Fay* is still in LSWR livery. (AC)

Right:
Second series Eastleigh 'Arthur' No E798 *Sir Hectimere*, as built. The locomotive is coupled to an Ashford-pattern 3,500-gallon tender which is narrower than the locomotive cab. The drawgear and running-plate are higher than the Eastleigh standard, so the second batch of Eastleigh 'Arthurs' were built with a shallower drop in the running-plate valance below the cab. (IA)

Right:
No 793 *Sir Ontzlake* in as-built condition at Bricklayers Arms. Eastleigh reverted to LSWR-style buffer beam numerals for this batch of 'King Arthurs'. The cylinders of this batch were fitted with piston tailrods. Note the pipes from the cylinder drain cocks are extended forward and fixed to the back of the footstep backing plate. Piston tailrods were a feature of Maunsell 'N' class 2-6-0s and Urie's first batch of 'H15s' but this was the only batch of 'King Arthurs' to be so fitted. (WJR)

Right:
No E796 *Sir Dodinas le Savage* departs Victoria on a Brighton train. The overhead wires for the LB&SCR suburban electric services are still in place. The visible coaches are LB&SCR high-roofed 'Balloon' stock of 1905. (RG)

24

Left:
No 836, a Maunsell 'S15' class built in 1927 and initially painted in black with green lining. A boiler with multiple washout plugs is fitted. The locomotive was built with plain lamp irons and curved footstep backing plates. No 836 is coupled to a flat-sided bogie tender. Between 1930 and 1941, all 'S15s' were painted green but then repainted in unlined black. (AC)

locomotives from the takeover of the Plymouth, Devonport & South Western Junction Railway and the Lynton & Barnstaple Railway. Badly in need of work, NBL had tendered a low price (£7,780) for each locomotive. There must have been massive pressure on the workforce from management to get the order built on time and to budget. There were some problems with poor workmanship, also initial performance did not match that of the Eastleigh 'Arthurs'. Once overhauled at Eastleigh, the 'Scotchmen' came up to expectations.

THE SECOND SERIES EASTLEIGH ARTHURS (OR BRIGHTON ARTHURS)

In 1925/6, a further order for 25 'King Arthurs' was placed with Eastleigh Works. However, only 14 were built, the other 11 being replaced by Maunsell's larger four-cylinder 'Lord Nelson' class locomotives. The 14 built worked the central section, and were fitted with Ashford-pattern 3,500-gallon (15,911-litre) tenders. The running plate and drawbar of these tenders was higher than the LSWR standard which had been used on all 'King Arthurs' built. So the locomotives were built to suit, with a higher drawbar and with a shallower drop to the running plate below the cab, to match the Ashford-pattern tenders.

To match the style of the tender, the backing plates of the footsteps below the front buffer beam and the cab now had the inner edge shaped in a continuous curve, in place of the vertical edge with a sharp curve at the bottom as on previous 'King Arthurs'. The cut out at the ends of the buffer beam was larger and there was no fillet to the front or rear of the running plate valance.

This batch of 'King Arthurs' was built with piston tailrods to the cylinders, a feature of Maunsell's 2-6-0 and 2-6-4T designs, but were not fitted to any of his 4-6-0s except for this batch. The tailrods were removed within a few years. The pipes from the cylinder drain cocks were extended forward to be fixed to the footstep backing plates, a modification which was applied to the rest of the Urie/Maunsell 4-6-0s during the 1930s.

THE MAUNSELL S15S

Having made a brief mention of the other varieties of Urie 4-6-0s in the Introduction, the story may be completed by a brief mention of the further examples of the small-wheeled 'S15' class built under Maunsell's control. Twenty-five locomotives, Nos 823 to 847, were built at Eastleigh between 1927 and 1936. All incorporated the improvements made to the Maunsell 'King Arthurs' and were built to the SR composite loading gauge.

The boilers of the 'S15s' were interchangeable with those on the 'King Arthurs', but boiler Nos 833 to 841 and spare boiler No 1057, had a different arrangement of washout plugs. All the Urie boilers, and most of the Maunsell boilers, had two washout plugs on either side of the firebox above the handrail, those on the right side being set further forward than those on the left. These 10 boilers had four washout plugs on the right-hand side of the firebox and five on the left (the four being set opposite the gaps between the five plugs) and appeared from time to time on all types of 'King Arthurs'. Some boilers, including No 835 and No 1057, were later modified to the two-plug arrangement.

CHAPTER TWO

MODIFICATIONS

After modifications to bring the Urie-designed
locomotives closer to the standard of Maunsell's
'King Arthurs', further alterations carried out on the
class throughout service were fairly superficial.

Over the years a number of modifications, some temporary others permanent, were carried out to the 'King Arthurs'. The modifications are described in the order in which they were first carried out; the first modifications were applied only to Urie 'Arthurs'. The tables in the Appendices show, where known, the dates at which modifications took place.

OIL BURNING

There were three occasions on which Urie 'Arthurs' ran briefly as oil burners. During a coal strike in 1921 and during the General Strike in 1926 two locomotives (below) ran with this equipment. A rectangular oil tank was mounted in coal space of the tender:
No 737 from 23 April to 26 September 1921 and from 16 June to 22 December 1926;
No 739 from 18 June to 6 August 1921 and from 12 June to 17 December 1926.

Due to a coal shortage after World War 2, a Government scheme was brought in to convert large numbers of locomotives to oil burning. On the Southern, these included five Urie 'Arthurs' (see table below), which were also fitted with electric lighting to the locomotive and tender. This equipment was retained after reverting to coal burning, together with the tubular ladders (which had been added at the rear of the tenders) below the framing at the side and on the rear of the tender tank.

FEEDWATER HEATERS

Some of the Urie 'Arthurs', thought to be Nos 736 to 745, were initially provided with cylindrical feedwater heaters, mounted transversely between the two bogies of the tender. The heaters are only visible if the tender is seen broadside on and were soon removed by Maunsell.

Locomotive	Oil Burning	Electric Lighting	Coal Burning
No740 *Merlin*	14 December 1946	3 January 1948	30 October 1948
No745 *Tintagel*	4 October 1947	4 October 1947	18 December 1948
No748 *Vivien*	27 September 1947	13 December 1947	20 November 1948
No749 *Iseult*	11 October 1947	28 November 1947	20 November 1948
No752 *Linette*	27 September 1947	20 December 1947	25 September 1948

Above:
Urie 'N15' class
No 737 *King Uther*
at Eastleigh, fitted for
oil burning between
23 April and
26 September 1921.
The photograph
shows the feedwater
heater positioned
between the tender
bogies. This was
removed, probably
very early in Southern
Railway days. (AC)

Left:
Urie 'N15' class
No 739 *King
Leodegrance* at
Eastleigh, fitted for
oil burning between
18 June and
6 August 1921. (AC)

Top:
Oil burning No 749
Iseult at Eastleigh,
4 September 1948, in
Malachite Green.
Electric lighting is
fitted, as are tubular
ladders at the rear
of the tender.
(AEW/SWC)

Above:
Oil-burning 'Arthurs'
No 749 *Iseult* and
No 748 *Vivien* at
Eastleigh, 11
September 1948.
Both were converted
back to coal burning
in November 1948.
(HC)

BOILER CHANGES

The Urie 'Arthurs' were delivered with coned boilers, working at a pressure of 180psi (12.2 Bar). Similar boilers were provided for the Urie 'S15s' and the 1924-built batch of 'H15s'. The Maunsell boilers, used on the Eastleigh 'Arthurs', 'Scotchmen' and Maunsell 'S15s' were dimensionally identical but worked at a pressure of 200psi (13.6 Bar). The only visible external difference between the two types was that the Maunsell boilers had Ross Pop safety valves on a low casing in place of the encased direct loading valves fitted on the Urie boilers.

LSWR practice was to have the same number of boilers as locomotives with the result that overhaul duration was governed by the time taken to remove, overhaul and re-fit the boiler. Maunsell's practice was to have additional spare boilers, allowing overhaul times to be reduced by fitting boilers which had already been reconditioned. Spare Maunsell boilers were fitted to No 737 *King Uther* and No 742 *Camelot* in October and December 1925, both with Urie-type superheater and smokebox doors. Over the years, all the Urie 'Arthurs' except No 749 *Iseult* and No 755 *The Red Knight* ran with Maunsell boilers at some stage. 'Scotchman' No 799 *Sir Ironside* also ran for a time with a Urie boiler.

In the late 1920s, a number of new boilers were built with a different arrangement of washout plugs on the firebox. These were initially fitted to new 'S15s', but later appeared from time to time on all varieties of 'King Arthur'.

SUPERHEATER

The Urie 'Arthurs' all entered service with the Eastleigh-type superheater fitted. These were replaced with the Maunsell-type superheater between 1928 and 1932, the change being

Left:
In late 1925, some new Maunsell boilers were supplied by NBL as exchange spares to speed up overhaul time. Two were fitted to Urie 'Arthurs' Nos E737 *King Uther* and E742 *Camelot* and had the Eastleigh-type superheaters. Snifting valves were not fitted. No E742 *Camelot* is seen at Nine Elms. (IA)

Left:
No 800 *Sir Meliot de Logres* in the 1930s. The E-prefix was removed in November 1932. Piston tailrods have been removed and replaced by a bolted cap. No 800 is fitted with one of the boilers built for 'S15' class 4-6-0s Nos 833 to 841 in 1928. The pipes from the cylinder drain cocks, are now fixed to the front face of the steps. The original lamp sockets across the buffer beam all contain lamp irons. (AC)

Left:
No 799 *Sir Ironside* at Ramsgate, the only example of a Maunsell 'King Arthur' to run with a Urie boiler from November 1934 to August 1937. (AC/RKB)

apparent by the provision of a pair of snifting (anti-vacuum) valves at the rear of (high up) the smokebox. The Eastleigh 'Arthurs' and 'Scotchmen' were all built with the Maunsell-type superheater. Bulleid had the snifting valves removed between 1947 and 1950. A Bolton-type superheater was fitted to one boiler, which was carried by No E455 *Sir Lancelot* from July 1929 to February 1931 and by No E454 *Queen Guinevere* from May 1931 to August 1932. It is not known whether the snifting valves were retained for this type of superheater.

WORKS PLATES

When new, 'Scotchmen' were fitted with circular North British Locomotive Co (Hyde Park Works) plates mounted on the side of the

smokebox, above the steam pipe cladding. Photographs of 'Scotchmen' without smoke deflectors all show the works plates in place, but they were hidden when smoke deflector plates were fitted. The plates were probably removed when new smokeboxes were required.

CHIMNEYS

The 'Urie Arthurs' were built fitted with a stovepipe-type chimney and capuchon. During the tests to improve steaming, No E742 *Camelot* ran between July 1924 and December 1925 with a tall, lipped chimney. At an unknown date between 1925 and 1927, No E755 *The Red Knight* ran with a stovepipe-type chimney with a reduced size capuchon and also a louvre in the front of the chimney. Between 1925 and 1929,

Left:
Urie 'Arthur' No E753 *Melisande* fitted with a steel strip across the front of the smokebox, which was carried between 21 May and 16 June 1926. 'Scotchman' No E774 *Sir Gaheris* was fitted with a similar device. (AC)

Far left:
Eastleigh 'Arthur' No E450 *Sir Kay* at Nine Elms. Small wing plates, connected at the back, are fitted behind the chimney. The plates were carried between February 1926 and March 1927. (AC)

Left:
'Scotchman' No E772 *Sir Percivale* with the large German-type smoke deflectors fitted from September 1926 until October 1932. The deflectors were similar to those on the German State Railways Class 01 and 02 Pacifics of 1925. (IA/PRW)

Far left:
Eastleigh *'Arthur'* No E453 *King Arthur*, with short smoke deflectors as fitted between April 1927 and July 1928. The top of the deflectors are fixed to the boiler handrail. (IA)

all received standard 'King Arthur'-type lipped chimneys, which were lower than that on No E742 to fit the SR composite loading gauge. No 747 *Elaine* ran with a shorter 'Lord Nelson'-type chimney between 30 November and 6 December 1937. The very short period of use suggests that it ruined the steaming qualities of the locomotive.

Bulleid fitted the following Urie 'Arthurs' with the wide Lemaître-type multiple blast pipe chimney, which had vastly improved Maunsell's 'Lord Nelson' class:
No 736 (December 1940), No 737 (February 1941), No 741 (December 1940), No 752 (February 1941), No 755 (February 1940)

No 755 *The Red Knight* also had 1ft 10in (55.9cm) Bulleid-designed cylinders and became a 'Super Arthur'. However these cylinders, as well

as the Maunsell-designed double ported type, did not look any different from the Urie-type so are not listed in detail. A Lemaître chimney was also fitted to 'Scotchman' No 792 *Sir Hervis de Revel* between September 1940 and 1 March 1952, after which the Maunsell-type chimney was refitted.

In late 1940, trials were carried out on No783 *Sir Gillemere* to disperse the exhaust steam and make the locomotive less visible from the air. Three arrangements were tried:
November and December 1940. Three stove-pipe chimneys, two side-by-side and one central to the rear.
December 1940 and January 1941. Rear chimney removed, the front two extended in height.
January and February 1941. Plates fitted between the smoke deflectors and the smokebox,
February 1941. Normal chimney refitted,

Above:
During the six years of running with German-type smoke deflectors, No E772 was fitted with four different tenders. In November 1928, it was coupled to a 4,000-gallon six-wheeled tender. Note that the curved plates of the front drop have been replaced (or covered over) by straight angled plates, with an inset footstep. This was also copied from the German Pacifics. (IA)

Right:
No E783 *Sir Gillemere,* with the shovel-shaped device around the chimney, which was fitted from March to December 1927. The location is Oxford, 9 May 1927. (HC)

Far right:
No E779 *Sir Colgrevance* was the first 'King Arthur' to be fitted in April 1927 with what became the final pattern of smoke deflectors. On E779, either the cladding over the steam pipes was cut back or the deflector plates were closer to the edge of the running plate than standard. (IA)

Large-diameter tapered chimneys with spark arresters were fitted to No 784 from June 1947 to May 1948, later as No 30784, from February 1949 to October1954 and to No 30788 from December 1949 to June 1951.

SMOKE DEFLECTORS

During the 1920s, problems occurred with the exhaust steam from the chimney clinging to the boiler and drifting around the cab obscuring the driver's view of the line. This was a problem which occurred on many locomotives with a large boiler and short chimney. Various experimental devices were tried, to provide an upward air flow past the chimney, and lift the exhaust clear of the boiler. These devices are listed in the order in which they were fitted.

The louvred chimney fitted on No E755 *The Red Knight* may have been an attempt to lift the exhaust clear of the boiler, or a means of providing an updraught when the regulator was closed.

In February 1926, Eastleigh 'Arthur' No E450 *Sir Kay* was fitted with two small wing plates behind the chimney which were totally ineffective and removed in March 1927.

Urie 'Arthur' No E753 *King Arthur* was fitted with a curved steel strip on the top of the smokebox front from 21 May to 16 June 1926. 'Scotchman' No E774 *Sir Gaheris* had a similar strip fitted at an unknown date.

In September 1926, 'Scotchman' No E772 *Sir Percivale* was fitted with large vertical smoke deflector plates mounted on the running plate and fixed to the smokebox by two large metal

straps. These followed the design of deflector plate fitted in 1925 on the Richard Wagner-designed Class 01 and 02 Pacifics of the German State Railways. The deflectors worked, but were considered to be unsightly, being retained until February 1932.

Between March and December 1927, No E783 *Sir Gillemere* was fitted with a shovel-shaped device around the chimney.

In April 1927, No E453 *King Arthur* had short plates fitted alongside the smokebox attached to the running plate and boiler hand-rail. The plates were partially effective and were carried until July 1928.

The standard smoke deflector plates, fitted to all the Urie/Maunsell 4-6-0s between 1927 and 1929, were a development of the plates on No E453 but were extended forward over

the front drop to the running plate. The plates were first fitted to No E779 *Sir Colgrevance* in April 1927, on which the forward extension was clearly an addition to the short plates. No E749 *Iseult* was fitted with similar plates in August 1927 and the remainder of the class from November 1927. On No E779, the cladding over the live steam pipe did not project through the smoke deflector plates. On all the others, the smoke deflector plates were cut out to clear the cladding over the steam pipe. When these plates were fitted, the wide footsteps on the front drop to the running plate were removed. Some of the first locomotives to be fitted with smoke deflectors initially had no step at this location and no handhold on the front edge of the smoke deflector. Narrow steps, bracketed to the outer

Right:
No E784 *Sir Brian*, in partly stripped condition at Eastleigh, 12 August 1928. The removal of the steam pipe and snifting valves suggests that the superheater has been removed. The removal of the cab roof and the row of open rivet holes at the rear of the smokebox suggest that E784 has just had, or is about to have, a boiler change. The North British works plate is still on the smokebox, but it is likely that this plate would not be replaced when a new smoke-box was required. (HC)

Right:
No E773 *Sir Lavaine*, fitted with a circular-shaped hood, projecting forward from the upper part of the smokebox. Nothing is known about this arrange-ment which was carried briefly. Two years later No E773 was fitted with standard smoke deflectors. The smokebox side lamp irons are in the later position on the smokebox door, but the top iron has been repositioned onto the hood. The smokebox door handrail has been shortened. The NBL plate appears to be on the side of the smokebox. The wide footsteps on the front drop and the short grab rail on the outside of the main frame have been refitted. *Sir Lavaine* is approaching Woking on a Southampton train via Alton, 17 May 1930. (HC)

face of the smoke deflectors, and handholds in the deflector were fitted later. Photographs confirm that locomotives initially without steps and handhold included Nos 451, 752, 765, 777, 779 and 780. It is likely that all locomotives shown in the Appendix as having received smoke deflectors during or before December 1927 were initially without steps and handholds.

'Scotchman' No 773 *Sir Lavaine* ran with a circular projection ahead of the smokebox, for an unknown period around 1930. It is not known whether this was another smoke deflector trial or it was for some other purpose.

After being fitted with the Lemaître-type exhaust, Nos 736, 752 and 755 were fitted with vertical set smoke deflectors in May 1949, December 1947 and January 1945 respectively. Those on Nos 737, 741 and 792 were not altered.

SMOKEBOX DOORS & BOILER HANDRAILS

The Urie and Eastleigh 'Arthurs' Nos E448 to E457 were built with the Urie-pattern smokebox door, with a central closing dart and four dogs around the bottom of the door. The boiler handrail was continuous over the front of the smokebox. When requiring replacement, the Urie-type was replaced by the Maunsell-pattern door which had longer arm hinges, no central dart, six closing dogs and a horizontal handrail. The dates of these replacements are not known, but occurred after the fitting of smoke deflectors at the same time the boiler handrail was fixed to the top of the smoke deflector. Where smoke deflectors were fitted to locomotives retaining the Urie-pattern smokebox door, the continuous handrail was usually replaced

Left:
No E452 Sir
Meliagrance
approaching
Earlsfield on a down
West of England
express circa 1930.
The usual arrange-
ment of smokebox
front handrail, used
on 'King Arthurs'
with smoke deflectors
and a Urie-pattern
smokebox door is
evident. The boiler
side handrail ends at
the smoke deflector
and a separate
handrail is provided
over the smokebox
door. The handrails
on the mainframe
have been removed,
but the short vertical
stanchions above the
buffers are yet to be
fitted. A three-coach
set of Maunsell
coaches, with large
luggage vans, is
coupled to a brake
composite. (IA)

Left:
Eastleigh 'Arthur'
No E448 *Sir Tristram*,
note the continuous
handrail is retained
and conventional
lamp irons have been
added to the sides of
the smokebox. The
handrails on the
mainframe have been
replaced by short
vertical stanchions
above the buffer
beam. No E448 was
fitted with smoke
deflectors in April
1929, and later
photographed at
Salisbury on 31 May
1929, fitted with the
earlier positioned
handrail. (SLS)

by a separate curved-shaped rail over the door.
The continuous handrail was retained on a few
locomotives, including Nos 448, 746 and 747.
No 448 *Sir Tristram* was photographed with both
arrangements.

A small number of 'Scotchmen' and second
series Eastleigh 'Arthurs' carried the Urie-pattern
smokebox door for a period. This is confirmed by
photographs of Nos 780, 795 and 805.

LAMP IRONS

LSWR lamp irons were made with a socket, into
which a mounting tongue on the lamp or route
indicator disc was fitted, whereas the SE&CR and
LB&SCR used conventional lamp irons, requiring
a socket on the lamp or route disc. All the 'King
Arthurs', including those for use on the eastern

and central sections, were originally provided with
LSWR-pattern lamp sockets. Three sockets were
fitted above the buffer beam, one over each buffer
and one over the coupling. A socket was fitted
either side of the smokebox, level with the
centreline of the smokebox. On 'King Arthurs'
with the Urie-pattern smokebox door the top
socket was fixed to the handrail, below the
chimney. On 'King Arthurs' with the Maunsell-
pattern smokebox door, the socket was fixed to the
front face of the smokebox. From around 1926,
photographs show conventional lamp irons
inserted into the LSWR-pattern sockets.

When standard smoke deflector plates were
fitted, the smokebox side lamp sockets were
replaced by conventional (mounted high up) lamp
irons. A disc placed on these irons must have been
right in the crew's line of sight! By the early 1930s,

Above:
No E780 *Sir Persant*
departs Waterloo on
the inaugural
'Bournemouth Belle'
service in July 1931.
The locomotive is
distinctly scruffy for a
prestige working and
is a rare example of a
'Scotchman' with a
Urie-pattern smoke-
box door. The buffer
beam numerals are in
serif-style characters
with the 'E' prefix.
Compared to the
locomotive, the train
is gleaming with
varnish and newly
painted white roofs,
including the newly
introduced Umber-
coloured cantrail
panels. The first car is
12-wheel brake No 40
of 1921, followed by
brand new all-steel
parlour car 84. (AC)

Above right:
No E805 *Sir
Constantine,* an
example of a second
series Eastleigh
'Arthur' with a Urie-
pattern smoke-box
door circa 1930. The
revised painting of
the cabside, with the
green only up to the
top of the cabside
cutout, is evident.
(SLS)

the three top lamp irons were all mounted on the
smokebox door, if this was of the later Maunsell
pattern. The buffer beam lamp sockets were also
slowly replaced by conventional lamp irons. On oil
burning locomotives with electric lighting, the
three lights across the buffer beam had disc irons
mounted on top. The three top electric lights were
on the periphery of the smokebox front (in the
pre-1930 lamp socket positions) leaving the
existing smokebox door irons for mounting discs.

SPEED RECORDER

Locomotives Nos E742 *Camelot* and 451 *Sir
Lamorak* were fitted with Flaman speed recorders
during indicator tests between 1924 and 1925.
Nos E452 *Sir Meliagrance* and E782 *Sir Brian* were
fitted with the same equipment from October
1927 to December 1930. The recorders were
removed, due to unreliability. In each case, a cable

ran up the outside of the cab on the fireman's
side. After the equipment was removed, the
fixing holes for this cable were plugged with
bolts. These remained in position until
withdrawal but were removed from No 30782
Sir Brian around the time it was painted with the
first small-size BR totem.

Flaman speed recorders were later fitted to
'King Arthurs' Nos 451, 457, 767, 779 and 793
between 1938 and 1939. The equipment was
removed between 1941 and 1942, leaving no
visible sign of fitment.

AUTOMATIC TRAIN CONTROL

In October 1931, No 774 *Sir Gaheris* was fitted
with Strowger-Hudd manufactured Automatic
Train Control (ATC) equipment for trials
near Byfleet, Surrey. The equipment was
mounted inside the cab on the driver's side.

A series of plugged holes indicated the location of the ATC equipment. The system, which was worked by magnets on the track, was not adopted by the Southern. The LMS installed the equipment on stretches of the London, Tilbury & Southend (LT&S) line. The ATC was developed in the 1950s into the Automatic Warning System (AWS) adopted throughout British Railways.

The AWS system was being installed on some lines of the Southern Region shortly before the last 'King Arthurs' were withdrawn. No 30802 *Sir Durnore* was the only 'King Arthur' to be fitted with AWS equipment in July 1960. The arrangement is likely to have been the same as that fitted to a number of 'S15s', with the equipment on the front of the cab on the driver's side, the battery box on the left-hand running plate alongside the firebox, and the receiver on the bogie with a shield mounted in front.

VACUUM PUMPS

All the Maunsell 'King Arthurs' had a crosshead-driven vacuum pump mounted below the left-hand lower slidebar. These pumps were removed early during World War 2. Photographs of Maunsell 'King Arthurs' in the pre-war Bulleid liveries all show the pumps still in place, but have been removed by the time the locomotives were painted in wartime black.

CONNECTING RODS

Most 'King Arthurs' were fitted with connecting rods with split big ends which lasted for the loco-motives' time in service. Around 1945, a number of connecting rods with plain-bushed big ends were manufactured at Eastleigh and were first fitted to No 785 in 1945. Later, Nos 454, 797, 770, 785 and 786 were fitted with the plain bushed-type.

Above:
Connecting rod big end, eccentric crank and eccentric rod of 'Scotchman' No 30783 Sir *Gillemere.* (AEW/SWC)

CHAPTER THREE

ALLOCATION & USE

Limited by weight to the main lines, 'King Arthurs'
were allocated at one time or another to
all three sections of the Southern Railway,
primarily for passenger workings.

Two of the 'King Arthur' types were always restricted to the western section by loading gauge constraints. The others were initially divided between all three sections but the central section locomotives were displaced to the east by electrification in the 1930s and the remaining eastern section locomotives were displaced to the west at the end of the 1950s.

THE URIE ARTHURS

The Urie 'Arthurs' were always allocated to the western section and were generally used on mainline passenger work but with some goods work, particularly night services. Generally the class was not run west of Exeter, Devon, although it was authorised to run as far as Meldon Quarry, Okehampton, Devon, in 1944. Occasionally 'Arthurs' did run over the central section and regularly worked through trains over the GWR to Reading and Oxford. Some of the sheds did not differentiate between Urie and Maunsell 'Arthurs' for rostering. In late 1942, Nos 739, 740, 742, 744, 747 to 751 and 754 were loaned to the LNER and stationed at Heaton (Newcastle), mainly working mainline goods trains in turns worked by 'B16s' and 'K3s', but also with some local passenger work. The locomotives were returned to the Southern in July 1943, when US-supplied 'S160' class 2-8-0s became available.

With the coming of the Bulleid Pacifics, the Urie 'Arthurs' tended to be used on less important services. Some spent the winters in store, as did many Maunsell 'Arthurs' in later years. The coming of the BR Standard class 4-6-0 locomotives took away more of the 'Arthurs' work and the class was withdrawn between 1953 and 1958.

THE EASTLEIGH ARTHURS

The Eastleigh 'Arthurs' were also always allocated to the western section, precluded from service elsewhere by the height of the cab. When new 'Arthurs' were allocated to Exmouth Junction (Nos 448 and 449), Nine Elms (Nos 450 to 452) and Salisbury (Nos 453 to 457) and quickly proved to be superior to the Urie 'Arthurs'. By the 1930s, all were at Salisbury and were generally associated with that depot.

Bulleid Pacifics and BR Standard class locomotives displaced from the eastern section by the electrification of the Kent coast line between 1958 and 1960 took over the Eastleigh 'Arthurs' duties and all were withdrawn between 1958 and 1962.

THE SCOTCHMEN

The 'Scotchmen' were allocated to both the western and eastern sections, the eastern section

Above:
No E765 *Sir Gareth* near Patcham, Sussex, on the up 'Southern Belle'. No E765 ran with a six-wheeled tender from January 1929 to December 1936 and was one of the last locomotives to have the E-prefix removed, in April 1933. The leading Pullman brake is one built after World War 1 on underframes from ambulance cars. The Umber-coloured cantrail panels on most of the Pullmans and the electric third rail suggest the date is circa 1931. (AC)

Left:
Firebox backplate of Urie 'Arthur' No 30752 *Linette*, showing the firebox door, regulator, water gauges, lubricator and assorted oil reservoirs. (AEW/SWC)

Above:
No E768 *Sir Balin* on a boat train comprising Continental stock and Pullman cars still in the red livery used on the SE&CR. (RG)

Right:
No 781 *Sir Aglovale* approaching Havant on the Saturday 13.50 Waterloo to Portsmouth harbour train, February 1937. The 'King Arthurs' were not generally associated with the Portsmouth direct line, more the preserve of Drummond class 'D15s', or 'Schools' class 4-4-0s. Electric services over the Portsmouth direct started in July 1937. (IA/GJJ)

locomotives being based at Battersea (Stewarts Lane) and used initially on Continental boat train services, later also on the Victoria and Charing Cross, London to Margate, Kent, express services. On the western section, 'Scotchmen' worked all the main lines and through trains to the North as far as Oxford but were uncommon on the Portsmouth line. With the introduction of the Bulleid Pacifics workings became more menial and, with the electrification of the Kent coast line, those eastern section locomotives which were not withdrawn were transferred to the western section. All were withdrawn from traffic between 1958 and 1962. No 777 *Sir Lamiel* was retained for preservation in the National Railway Collection at York, and was restored to Maunsell livery by the Humberside Locomotive Society. The locomotive has been steamed both on main lines and on preserved railways around the country. *Sir Lamiel* was later repainted in BR Dark Green.

THE SECOND SERIES EASTLEIGH ARTHURS

Locomotive Nos 793 to 796 were initially based at Battersea (Stewarts Lane), but not permitted on the line from Battersea Park into London (Victoria). With the line cleared for use by 'Arthurs', the whole batch were sent to Brighton working London (Victoria) express services to

Brighton and Eastbourne, Sussex. Displaced by the Brighton and Eastbourne electrification between 1932 and 1935, all were moved to the eastern section where the small tenders were adequate for the Continental boat trains and Kent coast expresses. With the Kent coast electrification, those which were not withdrawn were transferred to the western section. All were withdrawn from traffic between 1959 and 1962.

THE KING ARTHUR SHED ALLOCATIONS

Urie 'Arthurs'

No	1923	1928	1939	1944	1951	1957
736	Nine Elms	Bournemouth	Nine Elms	Eastleigh	Bournemouth	
737	Salisbury	Exmouth Jn**	Nine Elms	Eastleigh	Bournemouth	
738	Nine Elms	Nine Elms	Nine Elms	Exmouth Jn	Bournemouth	Eastleigh
739	Nine Elms	Salisbury	Nine Elms	Eastleigh *	Bournemouth	Bournemouth
740	Nine Elms	Exmouth Jn**	Nine Elms	Eastleigh *	Bournemouth	
741	Nine Elms	Nine Elms	Nine Elms	Eastleigh	Bournemouth	
742	Nine Elms	Nine Elms	Nine Elms	Eastleigh *	Bournemouth	Bournemouth
743	Nine Elms	Bournemouth	Exmouth Jn	Eastleigh	Bournemouth	
744	Salisbury	Exmouth Jn**	Exmouth Jn	Salisbury *	Feltham	
745	Salisbury	Nine Elms	Salisbury	Salisbury	Basingstoke	
746	Nine Elms	Exmouth Jn**	Salisbury	Salisbury	Eastleigh	
747	Nine Elms	Exmouth Jn**	Salisbury	Eastleigh *	Eastleigh	
748	Nine Elms	Nine Elms	Salisbury	Eastleigh *	Eastleigh	Nine Elms
749	Exmouth Jn	Salisbury	Eastleigh	Eastleigh *	Eastleigh	Basingstoke
750	Salisbury	Nine Elms	Eastleigh	Eastleigh *	Nine Elms	Nine Elms
751	Nine Elms	Salisbury	Eastleigh	Eastleigh *	Nine Elms	Basingstoke
752	Nine Elms	Nine Elms	Eastleigh	Eastleigh	Nine Elms	
753	Exmouth Jn	Nine Elms	Eastleigh	Exmouth Jn	Nine Elms	Basingstoke
754	Exmouth Jn	Salisbury	Eastleigh	Eastleigh *	Nine Elms	
755	Exmouth Jn	Nine Elms	Eastleigh	Nine Elms	Nine Elms	Basingstoke

* Locomotives loaned to Heaton (LNER) between late 1942 and July 1943.
   Some, such as 744, retained Heaton on their bufferbeams on return to the SR

** Exmouth Jn (Exmouth Junction)

Second Series Eastleigh 'Arthurs'

No	1926	1933	1937	1943	1951	1960
793	Brighton	Battersea	Battersea	Battersea	Battersea	Feltham
794	Brighton	Battersea	Battersea	Battersea	Battersea	Basingstoke
795	Brighton	Battersea	Ramsgate	Battersea	Battersea	Feltham
796	Brighton	Battersea	Ramsgate	Battersea	Dover	Salisbury
797	Brighton	Ramsgate	Ramsgate	Ashford	Dover	
798	Brighton	Ramsgate	Battersea	Ashford	Dover	Salisbury
799	Brighton	Ramsgate	Battersea	Ashford	Bricklayers A	Salisbury
800	Brighton	Ramsgate	Ramsgate	Ashford	Bricklayers A	Eastleigh
801	Brighton	Ramsgate	Ramsgate	Ashford	Bricklayers A	
802	Brighton	Ramsgate	Ramsgate	Hither Green	Ashford	Eastleigh
803	Brighton	Ramsgate	Ramsgate	Hither Green	Ashford	Eastleigh
804	Brighton	Ramsgate	Ramsgate	Hither Green	Ashford	Eastleigh
805	Brighton	Ramsgate	Ramsgate	Hither Green	Ashford	
806	Brighton	Ramsgate	Ramsgate	Hither Green	Hither Green	Eastleigh

Eastleigh 'Arthurs'

No	1925	1933	1937	1943	1951	1960
448	Exmouth Jn	Exmouth Jn	Salisbury	Salisbury	Salisbury	Salisbury
449	Exmouth Jn	Exmouth Jn	Salisbury	Salisbury	Salisbury	
450	Nine Elms	Salisbury	Salisbury	Salisbury	Salisbury	Salisbury
451	Nine Elms	Salisbury	Salisbury	Salisbury	Salisbury	Salisbury
452	Nine Elms	Nine Elms	Salisbury	Salisbury	Salisbury	
453	Salisbury	Salisbury	Salisbury	Salisbury	Salisbury	Salisbury
454	Salisbury	Salisbury	Salisbury	Salisbury	Salisbury	
455	Salisbury	Salisbury	Salisbury	Salisbury	Salisbury	
456	Salisbury	Salisbury	Salisbury	Salisbury	Salisbury	Basingstoke
457	Salisbury	Salisbury	Salisbury	Salisbury	Salisbury	Nine Elms

'Scotchmen'

No	1925	1933	1937	1943	1951	1960
763	Battersea	Battersea	Battersea	Battersea	Battersea	Nine Elms
764	Battersea	Battersea	Battersea	Battersea	Battersea	Bournemouth
765	Battersea	Battersea	Battersea	Battersea	Battersea	Bournemouth
766	Battersea	Battersea	Battersea	Nine Elms	Battersea	
767	Battersea	Battersea	Battersea	Nine Elms	Battersea	
768	Battersea	Battersea	Battersea	Nine Elms	Battersea	Eastleigh
769	Battersea	Salisbury	Battersea	Battersea	Battersea	Eastleigh
770	Battersea	Battersea	Dover	Nine Elms	Dover	Eastleigh
771	Battersea	Battersea	Dover	Nine Elms	Dover	Bournemouth
772	Battersea	Battersea	Nine Elms	B'mouth*	Dover	Bournemouth
773	Nine Elms	Nine Elms	Nine Elms	Salisbury	Dover	Eastleigh
774	Nine Elms	Nine Elms	Nine Elms	Salisbury	Dover	Nine Elms
775	Nine Elms	Nine Elms	Nine Elms	Exmouth Jn	Dover	Feltham
776	Nine Elms	Nine Elms	Nine Elms	Nine Elms	Dover	
777	Nine Elms	Nine Elms	Nine Elms	B'mouth*	Battersea	Feltham
778	Nine Elms	Nine Elms	Nine Elms	Battersea	Battersea	
779	Nine Elms	Nine Elms	Nine Elms	Battersea	Battersea	
780	Nine Elms	Nine Elms	Nine Elms	Nine Elms	Nine Elms	
781	Nine Elms	Nine Elms	Battersea	Battersea	Nine Elms	Bournemouth
782	Nine Elms	Nine Elms	Battersea	Battersea	Bournemouth	Bournemouth
783	B'mouth*	B'mouth*	Battersea	Battersea	Bournemouth	Bournemouth
784	B'mouth*	B'mouth*	B'mouth*	B'mouth*	Eastleigh	
785	B'mouth*	B'mouth*	B'mouth*	B'mouth*	Eastleigh	
786	B'mouth*	B'mouth*	Exmouth Jn	Exmouth Jn	Eastleigh	
787	B'mouth*	B'mouth*	Exmouth Jn	Exmouth Jn	Eastleigh	
788	B'mouth*	B'mouth*	Exmouth Jn	Nine Elms	Eastleigh	Eastleigh
789	B'mouth*	B'mouth*	Exmouth Jn	Exmouth Jn	Eastleigh	
790	B'mouth*	B'mouth*	Exmouth Jn	Exmouth Jn	Eastleigh	Eastleigh
791	B'mouth*	B'mouth*	Exmouth Jn	Exmouth Jn	Battersea	Eastleigh
792	B'mouth*	B'mouth*	Exmouth Jn	Exmouth Jn	Battersea	

* Bournemouth

CHAPTER FOUR

TENDERS

'King Arthur' locomotives were built with three types
of tender and two more varieties appeared briefly in the late
1920s and 1930s fitted to a small number of locomotives.

E ach of the four batches of 'King Arthur'
were initially delivered with the same type
of tender fitted to all locomotives within a
batch. Apart from 10 locomotives, tenders
generally remained with the same locomotive
throughout service, until replacing of tenders
became common in the late 1950s.

URIE ARTHURS

The Urie 'Arthurs' were built with Urie-pattern
5,000-gallon (22,730-litre) bogie tenders built
to Eastleigh drawing No E-11925. Those fitted
to locomotives Nos 736 to 745 were originally
built with feedwater heaters mounted between
the two bogies on the tender, but these were
removed in early Southern days. The engine
record cards do not show a single tender change
to any Urie 'Arthur', until No 30755 *The Red
Knight* was fitted with the tender of No 30754
The Green Knight when the latter was withdrawn
from service.

The main visible change to the tenders on
Urie 'Arthurs' occurred during the periods when
some locomotives ran as oil burners. The tenders
equipped for oil burning in the late 1940s retained
electric lighting and rear ladders after the oil tanks
were removed. The lamp iron modifications as
described for the locomotives were also applied to
the rear of the tenders.

EASTLEIGH ARTHURS

The Eastleigh 'Arthurs' ran with the
Drummond-pattern 4,300-gallon (19,548-litre)
bogie tenders which had been fitted to the
'G14' and 'P14' class 4-6-0s. These were similar
to the 4,000-gallon (18,184-litre) tender used
on most of Drummond's 4-4-0s, but had an
additional tank mounted towards the rear on
the top of the tender. The number of coal rails
was increased from two to four allowing
5 tons (5,080.25kg) of coal to be carried.
When running with the Drummond 4-6-0s,
these tenders were fitted with feedwater
heating pipes in the water space and had
double skinned sides, to conserve the heat.
Photographs indicate that the outer skin was
removed when the tenders were overhauled
ready for use on Eastleigh 'Arthurs'. No E449
Sir Torre was the Southern Railway's exhibit at
the Stockton & Darlington Railway centenary
parade on 2 July 1925. For the event, it was
fitted with a Urie-pattern tender which was
retained at least until September 1925, when
Sir Torre was photographed at Nine Elms.

By the late 1950s, the Drummond-pattern
tenders were worn out and were replaced by
Urie-pattern tenders from other locomotives
which had been withdrawn. These were
mostly standard Urie-pattern 5,000-gallon

Above:
Urie 'Arthur'
No 30745 *Tintagel*
at Woking, 1955.
The locomotive
is carrying the
Southampton Docks
headcode, and the
train includes
Pullman cars.
However, it appears
to be more of a
special occasion
than an ordinary
boat train. (CR)

Left:
No E737 *King Uther*
at Eastleigh,
12 August 1928,
showing the number
plate on the rear of
the tender. This plate
was identical to those
on the cabside.
The lamp sockets
all contain lamp
irons. (HC)

Above:
Between 1931 and 1932, the five 'King Arthurs' with flat-sided bogie tenders had these exchanged for Urie-pattern tenders with additional vacuum reservoirs from 'LN' class 4-6-0s. No 769 *Sir Balan* is passing Bromley, 18 October 1936. (HC)

Centre:
No 764 *Sir Gawain* at Bournemouth West, circa 1935 showing the rear of the 4,000-gallon six-wheeled tender, fitted between April 1928 and November 1936. (IA)

Right:
No 777 *Sir Lamiel* at Bournemouth, 19 July 1937. When the E-prefix was removed, new cabside number plates were provided but the rear plates were replaced by transfer numerals. (HC)

Above:
No 804 *Sir Cador of Cornwall* at Salisbury, 20 July 1937. From the rear the width mismatch between the tender and the cab is very apparent. What was No 804 (a Ramsgate locomotive) doing at Salisbury? In July 1937, the locomotive was halfway between two Class A overhauls and may have been on test from Eastleigh after an intermediate (Class B) overhaul. (HC)

Centre:
No 450 *Sir Kay* in clean black livery at Exeter Central on an up train, 27 August 1945. The coal rails on Drummond tenders were plated during the 1930s. (HC)

Left:
No 449 *Sir Torre* in dirty black livery at Nine Elms 15 June 1946. The photograph shows clearly the arrangement at the front of the narrow-bodied Drummond-pattern tender. The widened running plate above the footstep was already there from 'P14' days. (HC)

Above:
No E768 *Sir Balin,*
with the new
4,000-gallon six-
wheel tender fitted,
from June 1928 to
January 1930, for
working on the
central and eastern
sections. (IA)

(22,730-litre) tenders as fitted to the Urie 'Arthurs' and 'Scotchmen' but No 30451 *Etarre* received the tender from 'Remembrance' class No 32332. This had initially been a standard Urie tender but, when attached to No 2332, the rebuilt LB&SCR 4-6-4T, in 1935 three vacuum reservoirs were fitted behind the coal space. Also curved footsteps at all four corners and a handrail above at the rear corners were fitted. When fitted to No 30451, the front footsteps were returned to the standard shape and the vacuum reservoirs removed, but the curved rear footsteps and handrails were retained. No 30457 was fitted with a 5,200-gallon (23,639-litre) tender from No 30490 a Urie 'H15'. This was 4in (10cm) narrower and 6in (15cm) deeper than the standard Urie-pattern 5,000-gallon (22,730-litre) tender, but otherwise identical.

SCOTCHMEN

The 'Scotchmen' were delivered with standard Urie-pattern 5,000-gallon (22,730-litre) bogie tenders. The North British Locomotive Company drawing for those fitted to the 'Scotchmen' is identical to those for the Urie 'Arthurs', apart from the omission of the feedwater heater between the two bogies and associated pipework. The bogie tenders were not necessary for the eastern section workings. In 1928 new six-wheeled 4,000-gallon (18,184-litre) tenders were provided for Nos 763 to 768 and Nos 770 to 772. In 1930,

No 768 and Nos 770 to 772 received new flat-sided 5,000-gallon (22,730-litre) tenders, to allow temporary loan to the western section. No 769 *Sir Balan* had already been transferred to the western section and also received one of the new tenders. No 769 had not been fitted with a six-wheel tender.

These two tender types were both new. The 5,000-gallon (22,730-litre) tender was a derivative of the Urie design, but with flat sides, including the coal retaining plates, following the style of the Ashford-pattern 3,500-gallon (15,911-litre) tender. These tenders had curved footstep backing plates at all four corners, and handrails at the rear corners. Three vacuum reservoirs were mounted behind the coal space. The bogies were similar to those on the Urie-pattern tenders, but with a deeper cutout in the sideframe between the axles.

The 4,000-gallon (18,184-litre) tender was a six-wheeled version of the flat-sided bogie tender. The underframe was totally different from the Ashford-pattern tender's slotted frame. These tenders also had footsteps at all four corners, but with straight backing plates. The drawbar and running plate height of both these tenders were to Eastleigh standard.

In 1931/2, locomotives Nos 768 to 772 received Urie 5,000-gallon (22,730-litre) bogie tenders which had been fitted to 'Lord Nelson' class 4-6-0s, so that the latter class could be fitted with the more 'modern looking' flat-sided tenders. These tenders were fitted

Left:
No 766 *Sir Geraint,*
with 4,000-gallon
six-wheel tender
fitted from January
1929 to July 1937.
The lamp irons are
now all on the
smokebox door and
the length of the
handrail has been
reduced. The short
stanchions above
the buffers are yet to
be fitted. The buffer
beam lettering is in
serif-style characters,
with 'Nº' to the left
of the coupling.
No 766 is at
Folkestone East
sidings in the 1930s,
waiting for a train
to be brought
up from Folkestone
harbour by an 'R1'
class 0-6-0Ts. (AC)

with three additional vacuum reservoirs mounted behind the coal space. The reservoirs were retained when the tenders were transferred to 'King Arthurs' and all had the modified bogie design, with deeper cut-out in the sideframes, as used on the flat-sided tenders. The tenders of Nos 30768, 30769 and 30771 retained the additional vacuum reservoirs until withdrawal. On locomotive No 30772 the reservoirs were removed during a general overhaul in February 1955 and those on No 30770 were removed around 1960.

Finally, between 1936 and 1937 Nos 763 to 767 were also transferred to the western section and were fitted with standard Urie-pattern tenders without the additional vacuum reservoirs, but not, as it happened, the same tender fitted in earlier service. These tenders had been fitted to 'S15s' in the meantime. The changes are listed in the table below.

A final relevant tender exchange was that No 30763 was fitted with a tender from a 'Remembrance' class in March 1956, with the minor differences described above for No 30451.

Tender	Urie 5,000-gallon (22,730 litre)	4,000 gallon (18,184 litre) six-wheel	5,000-gallon (22,730 litre) flat-sided tender	Urie 5,000-gallon (22,730 litre)
Locomotive				
No 763	May 1925	June 1928		October 1936
No 764	May 1925	April 1928		November 1936
No 765	May 1925	January 1929		December 1936
No 766	May 1925	January 1929		July 1937
No 767	May 1925	February 1930		June 1937
No 768	May 1925	June 1928	January 1930	March 1932
No 769	June 1925		December 1929	July 1931
No 770	June 1925	December 1928	May 1930	July 1932
No 771	June 1925	October 1928	May 1930	April 1932
No 772	June 1925	October 1929	July 1930	June 1931

SECOND BATCH EASTLEIGH ARTHURS

The second batch of Eastleigh 'Arthurs' were built with Ashford-pattern 3,500-gallon (15,911-litre) tenders originally designed for 'N' class 2-6-0s. The running plate and drawbar of these tenders were higher than the LSWR standard which had been used on all 'King Arthurs' built so far. The locomotives were built to suit with a higher drawbar, a shallower drop to the running plate below the cab and curved footsteps. The tenders were narrower than the locomotives. While the locomotives were allocated to the central and eastern sections, these small tenders were adequate. With the Kent coast electrification between 1959 and 1960, the remaining 'King Arthurs' on the eastern section were transferred to the western section where the tenders proved to be too small. Eight of the small tenders were replaced by Urie 5,000-gallon (22,730-litre) bogie tenders from withdrawn locomotives. The author does not know whether the locomotive drawbar was adapted to fit the tender, or vice versa. After this tender exchange, the running plate under the cab did not line up with that of the tender. Seven of the new tenders were standard Urie-pattern 5,000-gallon (22,730-litre), but No 30806 *Sir Galleron* was fitted with the tender from 'Remembrance' class No 32331 which had been modified with curved footsteps and additional vacuum reservoirs. When this was fitted to No 30806, the vacuum reservoirs were removed but the curved footsteps which matched the footsteps under cab of the locomotive were retained.

Above:
Bogie of tender No 887. It has the later pattern bogies with a deeper-shaped cutout between the axles, also different axlebox covers. (AC)

Above left:
The tender of No 30783, showing the mounting of the brake hangers. (AC)

Left:
Detail of tender No 866 on No 30752, showing the shovelling plate, handbrake and toolbox. (AC)

Centre left:
Urie tender No 859. It was rescued from Barry scrapyard. The tender floor and toolboxes are missing, showing the full length of the brake column. (AC)

Left:
Tender No 859 had been coupled to oil-burning equipped Urie 'Arthur' No 745. The electric lights and tubular ladders were removed when the tender was attached to 'S15' class No 30506. (AC)

Far left:
Rear of tender No 866 showing the electric lighting and tubular ladders. (AEW/SWC)

CHAPTER FIVE

LIVERIES & NUMBERS

Apart from the period 1942-46, when painted black,
the 'King Arthur' class was always painted green,
but with considerable variety in the shade and lettering

The Urie 'Arthurs' were delivered in the livery of the LSWR but by the mid-1920s all 'King Arthurs' were in the Southern's Dark Green livery. The wartime black period 1942-46 was preceded and followed by two periods of bewildering variety, until all settled down after 1950 to the BR standard Dark Green.

LSWR PASSENGER GREEN LIVERY

The Urie 'Arthurs' all entered traffic in the late LSWR Sage Green livery, finished with black edging and a fine white line. The number was applied to the cabside and to the locomotive and tender buffer beams in 6in (16.2cm) gilt lettering, shaded black. Buffer beam lettering consisted of 'Nº' to the left of the coupling and the number to the right. The tender was lettered 'L S W R' in 8^1/$_2$in (21.6cm) gilt lettering, shaded black. The Power Classification (A for all Urie/Maunsell 4-6-0s) was denoted by a small white letter on the running plate valance, by the front buffer beam.

MAUNSELL SR LIVERIES

The first Southern Railway livery (carried by the 1924 batch of 'H15s') continued the LSWR Sage Green, but with the lettering described below, for the Maunsell Green livery. Initially, there was no number displayed on the cabside. It is likely that Urie 'Arthurs' shown in the Appendix as receiving Southern livery during 1924 would have carried this livery. In February 1925, Maunsell adopted a darker green. This was the livery in which all the Eastleigh and 'Scotch Arthurs' went to traffic.

Cab, splasher, footplate valance and tender sides excluding the coal retaining rails or plates of Drummond and Urie tenders, were green, with a fine white line between the green and the black edging. On the Urie 'Arthurs' and the first series of Eastleigh 'Arthurs' there was a clear demarcation between the green cabside and black roof. On the 'Scotchmen' and the second series Eastleigh 'Arthurs', the cabside merged into the roof with a rainstrip at the level where the cab roof extended back over the tender fallplate. The cab roof below the rainstrip was initially green, with the top white line adjacent to the rainstrip. Around 1930, the white line was moved down to the level of the top of the cabside cutout and the roof above was painted black. Boiler bands were black with a fine white line either side, but with only one white line at the rear of the smokebox. Similar banding was applied to the front and rear vertical edges of the green-painted cylinder jackets, but this was replaced by a rectangular panel in the late 1930s. Wheels were painted green with black tyres and axle ends. In the mid-1930s, colour photography begins to appear so this livery is well recorded.

Above:
No 483, a Urie 'H15', after overhaul at Eastleigh, April 1938. The livery arrangement is identical to that carried by the 'King Arthur' class at the time and is by far the best colour portrait of the livery. The cylinder jackets are now lined out with a panel, in place of the double lining. (CR)

Left:
No 742 *Camelot,* a Urie 'Arthur', has just taken over the Birkenhead-Bournemouth through train from GWR No 5044 *Earl of Dunraven* at Oxford in April 1939. (CR)

Right:
No 456 *Sir Galahad* backing onto the 15.00 West of England express at Waterloo, June 1937. The locomotive has a Maunsell-pattern smokebox door and a full set of conventional lamp irons. The door handrail has been shortened, and the pipes from the cylinder drain cocks extended. The cylinder jacket is lined out with a panel replacing the two vertical double lines. (IA)

Right:
No 773 *Sir Lavaine* at Bournemouth Central in the late 1930s finished in Maunsell livery but the cylinder jacket is lined out with a panel. The smokebox door handrail is shortened and the pipes from the cylinder drain cocks are extended forward to the footstep. (AC)

Right:
No 782 *Sir Brian* was repainted in Maunsell green, with Bulleid-style lettering, February 1939. Apart from the lettering, the livery and lining remain as standard but the cylinder jackets now in black. (HC)

Left:
Urie *'Arthur'* No 752 *Linette*, repainted in Maunsell Green with Bulleid-style lettering, is about to depart Bournemouth Central on an up train, March 1939 . (AC)

Left:
Urie *'Arthur'* No 743 *Lyonnesse*, in Maunsell Green with Bulleid-style lettering, near Tisbury, Wiltshire on an up freight, 30 August 1940. The locomotive has been fitted with blackout curtains which are stowed on a frame at the front of the tender. (HC)

Left:
No 766 *Sir Geraint* at Folkestone junction, 25 June 1939. It had been repainted in Malachite Green with black edging and white lining in March 1939. The smoke deflectors and tender coping are black and the footsteps backing plates are green. The crosshead-driven vacuum pump is still in position. (HC)

The Southern Railway did not initially renumber 'acquired' locomotives, but added a prefix to the number, A (Ashford) for ex-SE&CR locomotives, B (Brighton) for ex-LB&SCR locomotives and E (Eastleigh) for ex-LSWR locomotives. New locomotives were numbered into the appropriate series by design, all the Maunsell derivatives of Urie designs having E prefix numbers. In 1931, the Southern abandoned prefixes, E series locomotives retaining their existing numbers whilst 1000 was added to most A series numbers, 2000 to B series numbers and 3000 to LSWR '0xxx' series numbers.

Initially, the Southern retained the LSWR-style gilt buffer beam numerals. The 'Scotchmen' were delivered with 6in (15.2cm) yellow serif numerals, but Eastleigh continued to use the gilt numerals on the second series Eastleigh

'Arthurs' and on repaints. Around 1928, the gilt buffer beam lettering was replaced by 6in (15.2cm) yellow serif numerals with the E prefix to the left of the coupling and the number to the right. When the prefixes were abandoned the 'Nº' reappeared on the buffer beams, to the left of the coupling.

The cabside numerals were replaced by cast oval brass numberplates, 13⅝in (34.6cm) x 7⅝in (19.4cm) with the lettering 'SOUTHERN RAILWAY' in an arc around the top of the plate with the number below and the prefix between. A third plate was attached to the rear of the tender body. When the prefixes were abandoned the cabside plates were replaced by plates with 'SOUTHERN' in an arc at the top, 'RAILWAY' at the bottom and the number in the centre. The numberplates fitted on the rear of the tenders

Right:
Urie 'Arthur' No 755
The *Red Knight*, with
Lemaître exhaust
fitted in August 1942.
It is painted in the
unlined black livery
used on all 'King
Arthur' repaints
between June 1942
and March 1946.
Lettering is Sunshine-
style in golden yellow
with green shading.
The blackout curtain
and frame are at
the front of the
tender. The location
is Nine Elms, 27 April
1943. (IA)

Right:
No 782 *Sir Brian*
near Fleet on an
up boat train from
Southampton docks
circa 1947. No 782
is still in wartime
black livery, but
that has not stopped
yard staff keeping it
clean. The leading
Maunsell brake
composite is in
Bulleid livery. (IA/CJG)

were replaced by transfer-applied numerals. The backing colour of the number-plates was initially either green or black but around 1926 it was red, using the same vermilion colour (with a hint of orange) as was used for the buffer beams. When nameplates were first applied to the Urie 'Arthurs', they were also initially either green or black backed, except for No E755 *The Red Knight*, which was always red backed. By the time the 'Scotchmen' appeared, nameplates were all backed in red, and remained so into early British Railways days.

Tender lettering comprised the word 'SOUTHERN', 9ft 9in (297.2cm) long in elongated 6½in (16.5cm) serif letters. The locomotive number was applied below it in

1ft 6in (45.7cm) block figures with the 3in (7.62cm) E prefix in between. The lettering and numbers were in a primrose colour.

BULLEID LIVERIES

Between 1938 and 1942, Bulleid tried out an assortment of brighter liveries. He tried a couple of experimental styles on No 749 *Iseult* but, as it did not go into traffic in this state, they are not described further. Liveries listed by Don Bradley, from records made by George Woodward, are:

(a) Maunsell Green with black edging and white lining from November 1938 to June 1939
(b) Malachite Green with black edging and white lining, used in March 1939

Left:
After February 1944, Urie/Maunsell 4-6-0s were allowed to run between Exeter and Okehampton, Devon, primarily to work ballast trains from Meldon Quarry. The locomotives would have run tender first in one direction, until a new turntable was installed at Okehampton in 1947. This is the only photograph known to the author of a *'King Arthur'* west of Exeter, although GWR enthusiasts would say it is east of Exeter. The unidentified Urie *'Arthur'* is climbing from St David's to Central on a freight, certainly not Meldon ballast, banked by a 'E1/R' class 0-6-2T. The headcode is obscured by the darkness around the smokebox front; it may only be a transfer working from the GWR's Riverside yard. (AC)

(c) Olive Green with Dark Green edging and yellow lining, from April to June 1939

(d) Olive Green with black edging and yellow lining, from June 1939 to June 1940

(e) Malachite Green with black edging and yellow lining, from June 1940 to March 1942.

(f) Maunsell Green with green edging and yellow lining, two locomotives September 1940 and February 1941

(g) Unlined Malachite Green, one locomotive in May 1941

It would appear that some of the earlier Malachite Green repaints used a lighter shade of green than that used subsequently. Besides the colour and black and white photographs of

No 789 *Sir Guy* and a number of 'Schools' class 4-4-0s show a startlingly light shade. Unlined Maunsell or Malachite Green were standard on smaller passenger locomotives at this time. Due to the reduced activity of railway photographers during the World War 2, there are very few photographs known to the author showing 'King Arthurs' in liveries (d) and (e) and none showing liveries (c), (f) and (g). The following notes must therefore be treated with extreme caution.

With liveries (a), (b) and probably (c), the lining remained as on the Maunsell livery, but now with unlined black cylinder jackets, although the wheels and footstep backing plates remained green. Smoke deflectors remained black. The

Right:
Urie 'Arthur' No 755 The *Red Knight* at Salisbury, 20 May 1947. The Lemaître exhaust was fitted in February 1940 and the smoke deflector plates were reset to vertical in January 1945. No 755 was painted Malachite Green in April 1946, with black-shaded 'Sunshine'-style lettering. The blackout sheet is rolled up inside the cab roof, but the frame at the front of the tender has been removed . (HC)

Right:
Urie 'Arthur' No 743 *Lyonnesse* at Bramshot Halt, between Fleet and Farnborough, Hampshire, on a Southampton Terminus to Waterloo stopping train. No 743 was painted Malachite Green in December 1946. Note the number on the left-hand side of the buffer beam. Bramshot Halt, which served a golf course, closed in 1946. So presumably No 743 is not stopping. (IA/RFD)

Right:
'Scotsman' No 790 *Sir Villiars* was painted Malachite Green in September 1946. No 790 is near Millbrook on a down Bournemouth train, January 1947. (IA/FFM)

Left:
'Scotchman' No 774 *Sir Gaheris* at Nine Elms, April 1947. It was painted in Malachite Green livery, with green smoke deflectors and wheels, but black footstep backing plates in 1946. This was the site of the Southern's only wartime locomotive write off, No 458 a Drummond 'T14' class received a direct hit by a bomb in October 1940. (CR/HJ)

Left:
Urie *'Arthur'* No 740 *Merlin* at Eastleigh, 1948 fitted as an oil burner. The tender now has green coal retaining plates and black-shaded lettering used from 1946 on green locomotives. With oil-burning equipment electric lighting is fitted and also tubular ladders on the rear of the tender. (CR/HJ)

Left:
'Scotchman' No 787 *Sir Menadeuke* near Herne Bay on an up Ramsgate train in 1947. The train consists mainly of 8ft 6in wide coaches built for the eastern section in the 1920s, but the third looks like an 8ft-wide Hastings line coach. The width restrictions on most of the eastern section had been eased by this time so after 1933 only 9ft-wide coaches were built. (CR/FNR)

Right:
No 774 *Sir Gaheris* in Malachite Green near Fleet on a West of England express, 1947. The vacuum pump on the right-hand lower slidebar has been removed. At the front of the train is a brand new three-coach set of Bulleid coaches, with temporary ventilators above the windows pending delivery of the sliding lights. The rest of the train is Maunsell stock, including a restaurant pair. (IA/RFD)

Right:
No 740 *Merlin* near Winchfield on a down Bournemouth express, 9 May 1947. The locomotive is fitted with Maunsell boiler No 837, built in 1928 with five washout plugs on this side of the firebox. No 740 was painted Malachite Green in August 1946 and fitted for oil burning in December 1946. Electric lighting was fitted in January 1948. (IA/MWE)

running number was applied to the cabside in place of the plate and the word 'SOUTHERN' was painted centrally on the green panel of the tender side. The sans serif block letters were in gilt with a fine body colour line inside the letters. Numerals were shaded black and did not have a body-coloured inside line. The gilt was later changed to golden yellow.

With liveries (d) and (e), the turned in part of the smoke deflectors and the whole tenderside, including the coping and coal retaining plates of Urie tenders and the coping of the Drummond tenders, was now green. In all the Bulleid Green liveries, the green on the cabside extended only to the top of the cabside cutout. The word 'SOUTHERN'

on the tender was now level with the number on the cabside. In 1941, the lettering was changed to the 'Sunshine' style. Both the numerals and the word 'SOUTHERN' were now shaded, gilt characters with black shading on green locomotives and golden-yellow characters with green shading on black locomotives. The scarcity of photographs from this period precludes any totally authoritative statement on liveries, but it is not thought that the Sunshine lettering was used on repaints to livery (e) during the period 1941/2.

Between June 1942 and March 1946, all repaints were in unlined black with green shaded 'Sunshine' lettering. The 'SOUTHERN'

Left:
Sir Brian at Eastleigh, 29 August 1948, was one of two *'King Arthurs'* which were never painted Malachite Green after 1946. *Sir Brian* was the only *'Arthur'* to have the BR number on Southern black livery. It had been renumbered No 30782 in May 1948 and remained in this condition until October 1949, when it was repainted BR Dark Green and fitted with a smokebox numberplate. (WG)

Left:
No 30451 *Sir Lamorak* near Porton on an up west of England express, 13 August 1948. The locomotive was renumbered on Southern Malachite Green livery in July 1948. A Bulleid brake composite is at the front of the train and a Bulleid three-car set behind the two prewar thirds. (IA/ACC)

Left:
No 30785 *Sir Mador de la Porte* near Winchfield on a Bournemouth express, 20 April 1949. It was renumbered, with a smokebox number-plate, on Southern Malachite Green livery in August 1948. The visible part of the train is one of Bulleid's superlative six-coach Bournemouth dining sets of 1947.(AC)

Right:
No s747 *Elaine* at Yeovil Town, 15 September 1948. It is one of four 'King Arthurs' which ran in Malachite Green with s-prefix numbers and with BRITISH RAILWAYS lettering in 'Sunshine' style on the tender. (AEW/SWC)

Below:
Urie 'Arthur' No 30742 *Camelot* approaching Eastleigh on a down train, the locomotive has been photographed by Eastleigh shedmaster Stephen Townroe. Note the nameplate has a red background. (CR/ST)

Left:
Urie 'Arthur' No 739
King Leodegrance at
Winchester in 1938
on the 11.30am
Waterloo to
Bournemouth
service. The Maunsell
four-car set 204 has a
Maunsell restaurant
pair added. Note the
cylinder jacket on
No 739 is lined out
with a panel. (CR)

title on the tender was in line with the cabside
number. In the Appendices tables, it has been
assumed that black was applied at the next
A overhaul after June 1942.

From March 1946, Malachite Green began
to be used again, to livery variant (e) with black
shaded 'Sunshine'-style lettering. Wheels were
generally still painted green, but footstep
backing plates were now black. Some 'King
Arthurs' did not receive Malachite Green until
early British Railways days. Locomotives
No 782 *Sir Brian* and No 800 *Sir Persant*
were never painted in the post-war Malachite
Green livery.

Above:
'Scotchman'
No 30788 *Sir Urre of the Mount* was fitted with a spark arrester chimney from December 1949 to June 1951, and is painted in Malachite Green with Gill Sans-style lettering. The location is Bournemouth Central, circa 1950, and No 30788 will take a through train to the Western Region via Basingstoke and Reading. (DLB)

Left:
Second series *'Arthur'* No 30805 *Sir Constantine* at Hither Green, 10 June 1950. The locomotive was painted in Malachite Green with Gill Sans-style lettering in October 1948. (WG)

BRITISH RAILWAYS LIVERIES

For the first 18 months of British Railways ownership the livery applied to 'King Arthurs' was the Southern Malachite Green, but with various schemes of lettering. Generally, full repaints only occurred at full overhauls but partial repaints, such as adding 30xxx numbers, also occurred during light repairs at Eastleigh, Ashford and Brighton. Dates of renumbering were recorded on the Engine Record Cards. Four 'King Arthurs' Nos s453 *King Arthur*, s747 *Elaine*, s750 *Morgan le Fay* and s787 *Sir Menadeuke*, ran with s-prefix

Right:
Scotchman'
No 30791 *Sir Uwaine* at Eastleigh, shortly after being repainted in Malachite Green, December 1948. Note the green wheels and smoke deflectors. This was the first of the class to be repainted with an unlettered tender. The power classification A has been moved from the front of the running plate valance to the cabside, below the number. (DLB)

Right:
No 30454 *Queen Guinevere* at Eastleigh, 19 March 1949, in Malachite Green with green smoke deflectors and wheels but an unlettered tender. The patch over where the snifting valve was mounted is apparent. The locomotive is fitted with plain-bushed big end connecting rods. (DLB)

Right:
No 30801 *Sir Meliot de Logres*, at Eastleigh, 9 July 1940, finished in Malachite Green with black edging and yellow lining. Note the black wheels and smoke deflectors, also no lettering on the tender. This style was effectively to the standard specification for BR Dark Green livery. (HC)

numbers. Also No s754 *The Green Knight* was given a prefix, but this was removed before entering traffic as the tender had been lettered 'SOUTHERN'.

Until July 1949, repaints were in Malachite Green but with a variety of lettering arrangements:

- Malachite Green with 'SOUTHERN' tender lettering, January 1948
- Malachite Green with 'BRITISH RAILWAYS' in 'Sunshine' lettering, February – June 1948
- Malachite Green with 'BRITISH RAILWAYS' in Gill Sans lettering, July–December 1948
- Malachite Green with no tender lettering, December 1948–July 1949

The 'BRITISH RAILWAYS' in 'Sunshine' style was produced by using transfer letters where these were available from the existing 'SOUTHERN' transfers, with the others letters hand painted. The last 'King Arthur' to receive this style, No 30744 *Maid of Astolat*, had unshaded letters to the Bulleid form. The cabside numerals were in Bulleid numerals when 'Sunshine'-style lettering was used on the tender, and in Gill Sans numerals when the tender was lettered in Gill Sans or unlettered. Smokebox number plates were fitted from June 1948, but were also added during intermediate works visits to locomotives in the earlier liveries. Probably starting with the repaints with unlettered tenders, the A power classification was moved from the front of the running plate valance to the cabside, below

the number. The last four Malachite Green repaints, Nos 30743, 30773, 30786 and 30801, had black smoke deflectors and wheels.

From late July 1949, all repaints were in British Railways standard Dark Green (sometimes erroneously referred to as Brunswick Green) with orange and black lining. On the first Dark Green repaint, No 30783 *Sir Gillemere*, the cabside lining was carried up to the top of the cabside cutout as on the Malachite Green liveries. On later repaints the cab lining on 'Scotchmen' and second series Eastleigh 'Arthurs' ended below the line of bolts, halfway up the cab cutout, although the green extended up to the rainstrip on the cab roof. The full-depth lining was retained on Urie and first series Eastleigh 'Arthurs'. Splasher lining, with a single orange line, initially followed the Malachite Green arrangement, extending under the nameplate as far as the subsidiary class plate. On No 30453 *King Arthur*, with no subsidiary plate below the name, the lining went right through. On later repaints, from about 1958, the splasher lining had a square cut ending either side of the nameplate. When the Dark Green livery was introduced, the red paint used for buffer beams and as the backing colour of the nameplates lost the orange tinge. In 1952, British Railways headquarters ruled that all nameplates should have a black background. This ruling was generally followed for main works repaints until the early 1960s, but many of the running sheds still repainted the nameplate backgrounds in red.

Above:
No 30801 *Sir Meliot de Logres,* at Eastleigh, 9 July 1949, showing the application of the livery to the six-wheel tender and confirming that no number was painted on the rear of the tender body. (HC)

Right:
'Scotchman' No 30775 *Sir Agravaine* on a train of banana vans at Southampton Docks, in the early 1950s. No 30775 was painted BR Dark Green with the large-style totem in November 1949. A BR shedplate is now fitted at the base of the smokebox door. (IA)

Below:
No 30747 *Elaine*, a Urie locomotive, is seen at Nine Elms in the mid-1950s. It is now in British Railways standard Dark Green with the small first totem on the tender. The locomotive was withdrawn from service in October 1956. The nameplate background colour is black. (CR)

The large version of the early BR totem was used until February 1950, but No 30457 *Sir Bedivere* and No 30741 *Joyous Gard* had blank tenders at first. After February 1950, the small totem was used. Around the time the large BR totem was replaced by the smaller version, the A power classification was replaced by the 5P classification painted above the number. However, some photographs show a small totem still with the A power classification. British Railways standard oval-shaped shed plates were fitted to smokebox doors from around August 1950. These were fitted at running sheds as well as at works, so appeared fairly rapidly on all locomotives.

Some 'King Arthurs' of all varieties except the Urie 'Arthurs' later received the second BR totem from March 1957. This was applied with the heraldically incorrect right-facing lion on the right side of the tender until mid-1958. Left-facing lions were subsequently painted on both sides. The second totem was usually in the large size, but No 30453 *Melisande* received a small second totem in April 1957, to be repainted with a large totem in July 1958.

Right:
Urie 'Arthur'
No 30737 *King Uther*
at Eastleigh, 7 July
1951, is finished in BR
Dark Green, with the
small-style totem on
the tender. Apart from
the surviving GWR
'Star' class and
ex-GNR Pacific
No 60102, the first 17
Urie 'Arthurs' were the
only pre-Grouping
locomotives to be
painted in this livery,
within the 1949
range of the BR
standard liveries.
No 30737 is fitted
with a Urie boiler and
a Lemaître exhaust,
also standard angled
smoke deflectors.
The fluted slide bars
denote it to be one
of the first 10 Urie
'Arthurs'. (DLB)

Right:
'Scotchman'
No 30792 *Sir Hervis
de Revel* was the only
Maunsell 'King
Arthur' to be fitted
with a Lemaître
exhaust, September
1940 to March 1952.
It was repainted in
BR Dark Green with
the large-style totem
in March 1950. The
Southern power
classification A is now
on the cabside below
the number. (DLB)

Right:
Eastleigh 'Arthur'
No 30452 *Sir
Meliagrance* at
Eastleigh, May 1952
is finished in BR Dark
Green with small-
style totem. The A
power classification
has not yet been
changed to 5P. The
nameplate has a
black background.
(IA/GW)

Left:
Eastleigh 'Arthur' No 30451 *Sir Lamorak* passing Wilton, Wiltshire on an up train of containers in 1954, many years before Freightliner and block trains became the norm. The wagons are a mixture of flats, three-plank wagons and Conflats. No 30451 still has the Drummond tender. (IA/GFH)

Centre:
Eastleigh 'Arthur' No 30452 *Sir Meliagrance* at Exeter Central on an up train of ballast hoppers from Meldon, 3 July 1958. No 30452 was fitted with Urie tender No 902 in June 1957. The power classification is now shown as 5P, above the cabside number. The first hopper is one of the original batch of 40T wagons supplied to the LSWR by G.R. Turner of Langley Mill, Nottingham, in 1906. (IA/JS)

Left:
'Scotchman' No 30768 *Sir Balin* on a Victoria-Ramsgate express during the summer of 1957. The vacuum reservoirs at the back of the tender show that No 30768 was one of the 'Scotchmen' which had tender exchanges in the 1930s. Set 474 is basically a four-coach set, two brake thirds and two composites of high waisted Birmingham Carriage & Wagon-built Bulleid coaches, but has been made up to eight coaches by the addition of four BR-built Bulleid thirds. At least they are all green. (IA/PRW)

Above:
Eastleigh 'Arthur' No 30454 *Queen Guinevere* at Salisbury shed, October 1957. A standard Urie bogie tender was fitted in April 1957. Note the first style of BR totem on the tender. (CR/ID)

Right:
No 30450 *Sir Kay*, an Eastleigh 'Arthur', passing St James's Park Halt, Exeter, on an up express, August 1957. It must be a summer Saturday, and the train is probably one of the many portions of the up 'Atlantic Coast Express'. (CR/SW)

Above:
'Scotchman' No 30791 *Sir Uwaine* at Eastleigh, April 1957, carrying the headcode for a through train to the Western Region via Reading. (CR)

Left:
Second series Eastleigh 'Arthur' No 30803 *Sir Harry le Fise Lake* at Hither Green, March 1958. Hither Green provided motive power mostly for freight work but had one 'King Arthur' in the 1950s for a single Cannon Street-Ashford passenger working. (CR/WP)

Left:
Second series Eastleigh 'Arthur' No 30798 *Sir Hectimere* at Guildford, June 1962. Transferred to the western section after the Kent coast electrification, a Urie bogie tender is now fitted. If the date of the photograph is correct, the locomotive is almost out of service, being withdrawn on 16 June 1962. (CR/GHH)

73

Right:
Second series
Eastleigh 'Arthur'
No 30801 *Sir Meliot
de Logres*. It was
painted BR Dark
Green with the early
small-style totem in
1951. A Urie tender
finished with the
larger-style totem was
fitted in 1958. The
photograph is of
No 30801 shortly
after overhaul in
March 1954 as the 5P
power classification
is now, above the
number on the
cabside. (AC)

Right centre:
Second series
Eastleigh 'Arthur'
No 30796 *Sir Dodinas
le Savage* departing
Cannon Street on the
17.47 Ashford and
Dover service 30 May
1958, a week before
the change to diesel
operation. The
locomotive received
a repaint with the
second-style BR totem
in November 1957.
(IA/RCR)

Right below:
Second series
Eastleigh 'Arthur'
No 30799 *Sir Ironside*
was transferred to
the western section
after the Kent coast
electrification, and is
leaving Exeter Central
on the 10.27 to
Salisbury, 20 August
1960. It was with-
drawn, still with the
original small tender,
in February 1961.
Set 531 was one of
about 50 three-coach
sets of BR-standard
coaches supplied to
the Southern in 1955.
These were amongst
the last coaches on
the Southern to run in
Carmine and Cream.
(MJF)

Left:
Eastleigh 'Arthur' No 30457 Sir *Bedivere* at Nine Elms, 24 October 1959. It is fitted with one of the 1928 boilers with additional washout plugs and was fitted with the Urie 5,200-gallon tender from 'H15' class No 30490 in June 1955. The mounting bracket on the cross-head for the vacuum pump has been removed. (IA/CB)

Left:
Eastleigh 'Arthur' No 30451 Sir *Lamorak* at Eastleigh, 12 March 1961. No 30451 is photographed after the completion of the last general overhaul to be carried out on any 'King Arthur' class locomotive. The heraldically correct backwards facing lion is painted on the right side of the tender. The lining on the splasher has been simplified. Also the lining on the cylinder jackets is clearly visible. (IA/GW)

Left:
Second series Eastleigh 'Arthur' No 30793 Sir *Ontzlake* passing Esher, Surrey, June 1958. No 30798 was painted with the large BR second totem in June 1958. three-coach set No 565 has been made up to five with two green Bulleid thirds. (IA/GR)

Right:
No 30738 *King Pellinore.* This is one of the first batch of Urie 'Arthurs' (Nos 736 to 745), and is fitted with fluted slidebars. (AEW/SWC)

Right:
No 30754 *The Green Knight.* This is one of the second batch of Urie 'Arthurs' (Nos 746 to 755), and is fitted with plain slidebars. (AEW/SWC)

Right below:
'Scotchman' No 30783 *Sir Gillemere.* On all Maunsell-built 'King Arthurs' the slidebars were plain with tapered ends. According to the General Arrangement drawing, the reversing shaft was set 1in (2.5cm) further forward than on the Urie 'Arthurs', and the arm to the lifting link was 1in (2.5cm) longer, to increase valve travel. It needs the eye of faith to see any difference in the photograph. (AEW/SWC)

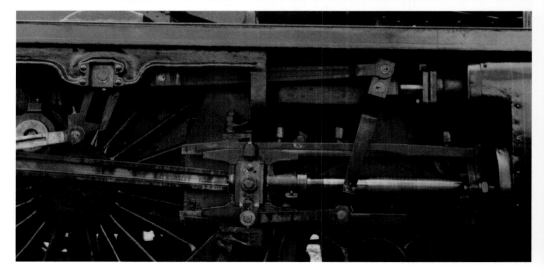

Left:
Motion on the driver's side of 'Scotchman' No 30783 *Sir Gillemere*. The lower slidebar has a thicker section where the vacuum pump had been mounted. Also there is an extension to the crosshead, drilled with four holes, where the pump drive had been mounted.(AEW/SWC)

Left:
Reversing rod and linkage on Urie 'Arthur' No 30752 *Linette*, showing also the steam powered turbo-generator for the electric lighting and the steam feed and exhaust pipes. (AEW/SWC)

Above:
Second series
Eastleigh 'Arthur'
No 30806 Sir
Galleron at Eastleigh,
21 July 1959. It was
fitted with a
Urie tender from
No 32331
'Remembrance' class
4-6-0 in September
1958. (IA/CB)

Right:
Second series
Eastleigh 'Arthur'
No 30806 *Sir
Galleron* leaving
Eastleigh on ballast
hoppers for the
Romsey, Hampshire,
line, 2 March 1960.
Most of the hoppers
are 40T bogie
wagons supplied
to the Southern
between 1928
and 1947. (IA/LE)

Above:
No 30765 *Sir Gareth* approaching Basingstoke on the 13.28 Lymington Pier-Waterloo, 18 August 1962. No 30765 was little used during the summer of 1962, but was steamed to replace the rostered 'Schools' class 4-4-0, which had failed. (AC)

Left:
No 30835, a Maunsell 'S15' at Basingstoke, 18 August 1962. This shows the arrangement of the BR Automatic AWS on these locomotives. The arrangement on No 30802, the only 'King Arthur' to be fitted, is believed to be the same. The receiver is mounted on the bogie, with a shield below the buffer beam to prevent contact with the coupling. The battery box is mounted on the running plate along-side the firebox. (AC)

CHAPTER SIX

NAMES

A newly appointed Public Relations Officer recommended
that the Southern Railway's new express locomotives
should carry names from the legends of
King Arthur and the Knights of the Round Table.

When the Southern Railway (SR) was formed, very few of its locomotives were named. There were dwindling numbers of LB&SCR express locomotives, most of which had the name removed at the first SR repaint. The naming of the Southampton Docks shunters was docks policy, not that of the LSWR. During the first year in business, the new SR received a very rough handling from the London press. General Manager Sir Herbert Walker appointed John Elliot, assistant editor of the *Evening Standard* (a London-based news-paper), to deal with the press and publicity. One of Elliot's first recommendations was to put names on the locomotives, suggesting the Knights of the Round Table for the new express types.

Who were King Arthur and the Knights of the Round Table? Arthur was almost certainly real. When the Romans began to withdraw their legions from Britain early in the 5th Century AD, the country was left without a trained army. Arthur was a British leader who had previously held a senior position in the Roman army, and had considerable success in stemming the tide of invaders from Northern Europe. He became a British (Welsh and Breton) folk hero and the tales of his exploits were passed down and

elaborated on over the centuries. Through Brittany the stories passed to Normandy, thence back to Britain. By the time Sir Thomas Malory translated the stories from French into English in 1469, myth had totally taken over from history and King Arthur is portrayed as King of 'England', the formation of which the real Arthur had been trying to prevent 1000 years earlier. Malory's *Le Morte d'Arthur* was the main source of the King Arthur names, but there are a few which must have come from elsewhere. The exploits of some of the knights are described in detail, but others are only mentioned as having participated in a particular battle or tournament. Most of Malory's women are nameless damosels or dames. The following notes are taken from a modern (1906) English translation of *Le Morte d'Arthur*. There are two Iseults, two Elaines, three Red Knights and three Sir Brians in the stories. In these cases, I have assumed that the locomotive names apply to the person not represented under another name.

After the Urie 'Arthurs' were withdrawn from service, their names were allocated to 20 British Railways Standard Class 5 4-6-0s, 73080-9 and 73110-19, which had taken over many of the 'King Arthur' duties. New plates, similar to the old ones but without the 'King Arthur Class' subsidiary lettering, were fitted between 1959 and 1961.

Above:
Sir Lamiel on the Severn Valley Railway at Bewdley, 8 May 1983. (AC)

Left:
In his book *Le Morte d'Arthur*, Sir Thomas Malory mentions a Sir Priamus. It appears as though one leg of the M became detached somewhere between John Elliot's clerk noting down the names from the book and the brass foundry at NBL. The nameplate is fixed by the correct pattern of bolt at the right-hand end but the other three are later replacements. (AC)

Left:
The nameplate of *King Arthur* was unique in not having the subsidiary 'King Arthur Class' lettering. (AC)

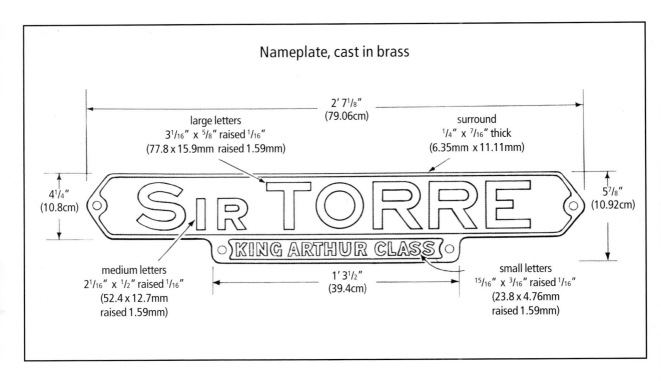

Nameplate, cast in brass

2' 7 1/8" (79.06cm)

large letters
3 1/16" x 5/8" raised 1/16"
(77.8 x 15.9mm raised 1.59mm)

surround
1/4" x 7/16" thick
(6.35mm x 11.11mm)

4 1/4" (10.8cm)

5 7/8" (10.92cm)

medium letters
2 1/16" x 1/2" raised 1/16"
(52.4 x 12.7mm
raised 1.59mm)

1' 3 1/2" (39.4cm)

small letters
15/16" x 3/16" raised 1/16"
(23.8 x 4.76mm
raised 1.59mm)

448 *Sir Tristram.* Son of King Meliodas of Liones and Elizabeth, sister of King Mark

449 *Sir Torre.* Son of King Pellinore by the wife of Aries the cowherd

450 *Sir Kay.* Son of Ector de Maris and foster brother of Arthur

451 *Sir Lamorak.* Son of King Pellinore and brother of Sir Percivale

452 *Sir Meliagrance.* Son of King Bagdemanus, with a castle near London

453 *King Arthur.* Son of King Uther and Igraine, fostered by Ector de Maris

454 *Queen Guinevere.* Daughter of King Leodegrance and wife of King Arthur

455 *Sir Launcelot.* Launcelot du Lac, son of King Ban of Benwick and lover of Guinevere

456 *Sir Galahad.* Son of Launcelot and Elaine. With Percivale, he sought the holy grail

457 *Sir Bedivere.* Threw Excalibur into the lake after Arthur's death

736 *Excalibur.* King Arthur's sword, pulled from a rock and thrown into the lake at the end

737 *King Uther.* King of England, father of Arthur. Took Igraine from the Duke of Tintagel

738 *King Pellinore.* King of the Isles, Father of Torre, Percivale, Lamorak and Aglovale

739 *King Leodegrance.* King Leodegrance of Camalaird, father of Guinevere

740 *Merlin.* Magician and manipulator (British fifth century bard Myrddin Emrys)

741 *Joyous Gard.* Launcelot's Castle, identified by Malory as Alnmouth or Bamburgh

742 *Camelot.* Arthur's city, identified by Malory as Winchester

743 *Lyonnesse.* Liones, part of Cornwall, Tristram's home

744 *Maid of Astolat.* Elaine, daughter of Sir Bernard of Astolat, died for love of Launcelot

745 *Tintagel.* Castle of King Mark of Cornwall

746 *Pendragon.* (Dragon's Head) Honorary title of King Uther

747 *Elaine.* Daughter of King Pellas, mother of Galahad by Launcelot

748 *Vivien.* From Tennyson's 'Merlin & Vivien', Malory's unnamed Lady of the Lake

749 *Iseult.* Fair Isout, wife of King Mark of Cornwall and lover of Sir Tristram

750 *Morgan le Fay.* Sister of Arthur, married to King Uriens of Gorre

751 *Etarre.* Ettard? Loved by Sir Pelleas until the Lady of the Lake took him on.

752 *Linette.* Daughter of Sir Persant, sister in law of Sir Gareth

753 *Melisande.* Perhaps from Maeterlinck and Debussy's 'Pélleas & Mélisande'??

754 *The Green Knight.* One of four brothers (Red, Green, Blue, Black), later Sir Pertolepe

755 *The Red Knight.* Another of the four, all beaten by Sir Gareth. Later Sir Perimones

763 *Sir Bors de Ganis.* Nephew of Launcelot, brother of Sir Blamore de Ganis

764 *Sir Gawain.* First son of King Lot of Orkney and Arthur's sister Margawse

765 *Sir Gareth.* Youngest brother of Sir Gawain, initially nicknamed Sir Beaumains

766 *Sir Geraint.* Garaunt? brother of Sir Guy and cousin of Guinevere

767 *Sir Valence.* Nearest match found in Malory is Sir Florence, son of Sir Gawain.

768 *Sir Balin.* Sir Balin le Savage, knight from Northumberland, brother of Sir Balan

769 *Sir Balan.* Brother of Sir Balin. As The Red Knight fought Balin and killed each other

770 *Sir Prianius.* Sir Priamus, Saracen knight fought by Gawain. ('m changed to ni')

771 *Sir Sagramore.* Sir Sagramore le Desirous, no further detail

772 *Sir Percivale.* Sir Percivale de Galis, son of King Pellinore, brother of Sir Lamorak

773 *Sir Lavaine.* Knight, name mentioned with no further detail

774 *Sir Gaheris.* Second son of King Lot of Orkney, Brother of Sir Gawain

775 *Sir Agravaine.* Third son of King Lot of Orkney, denounced Launcelot to Arthur

776 *Sir Galagars.* Knight, name mentioned with no further detail

777 *Sir Lamiel.* Sir Lamiel of Cardiff, name mentioned with no further detail

778 *Sir Pelleas.* Relative of King Ban, loved Ettard until entranced by the Lady of the Lake

779 *Sir Colgrevance.* Sir Colgrevance de Gorre, name mentioned with no further detail

780 *Sir Persant.* Sir Persant of Inde (Originally the Blue Knight, brother of Red and Green)

781 *Sir Aglovale.* Youngest son of King Pellinore

782 *Sir Brian.* Brian of the Forest, Brian of the Isles or Brian de Listonois?

783 *Sir Gillemere.* Sir Gilmere, name mentioned with no further detail

784 *Sir Nerovens.* Sir Nerovens de Lile, a knight of Sir Launcelot

785 *Sir Mador de la Porte.* Name mentioned with no further detail

786 *Sir Lionel.* Brother of Sir Bors and Sir Blamore, nephew of Sir Launcelot

787 *Sir Menadeuke.* Name mentioned with no further detail

788 *Sir Urre of the Mount.* A knight from Hungary, brought to Arthur's court badly wounded

789 *Sir Guy.* Sir Guy of Camiliard, cousin of Guinevere

790 *Sir Villiars.* Sir Villiars the Valiant, name mentioned with no further detail

791 *Sir Uwaine.* Son of King Urien of Gorre and Morgan le Fay

792 *Sir Hervis de Revel.* Name mentioned with no further detail

793 *Sir Ontzlake.* Brother of Sir Damas, who imprisoned Arthur and 20 knights

794 *Sir Ector de Maris.* Foster father of Arthur and father of Sir Kay

795 *Sir Dinadan.* Knight killed by Sir Agravaine and Sir Mordred

796 *Sir Dodinas le Savage.* Name mentioned with no further detail

797 *Sir Blamor de Ganis.* Nephew of Sir Launcelot and brother of Sir Bors

798 *Sir Hectimere.* Name mentioned with no further detail

799 *Sir Ironside.* Formerly the Red Knight of the Red Laundes, fought by Gareth

800 *Sir Meleaus de Lille.* Son of the King of Denmark

801 *Sir Meliot de Logres.* Wounded in a fight, but cured by Sir Launcelot with a sword

802 *Sir Durnore.* Name mentioned with no further detail

803 *Sir Harry le Fise Lake.* Name mentioned with no further detail

804 *Sir Cador of Cornwall.* Duke of Cornwall, father of Constantine

805 *Sir Constantine.* Son of Cador of Cornwall, became King after Arthur's death

806 *Sir Galleron.* Sir Galleron of Galway, name mentioned with no further detail

Plus three that never made it, and were renamed before entering service.

767 *Sir Mordred.* Son of Arthur by sister Margawse, denounced Launcelot to Arthur

787 *Sir Marmaduke.* Probably misreading of Sir Menaduke, (787 *Sir Menadeuke*)

788 *Sir Beaumains.* Nickname given to the young Sir Gareth (765) by Sir Kay

Urie 'Arthurs' - All built at Eastleigh Works

Number	736	737	738	739	740
Name	*Excalibur*	*King Uther*	*King Pellinore*	*King Leodegrance*	*Merlin*
Works Order No	N.15-1	N.15-2	N.15-3	N.15-4	N.15-5
To Traffic	31/8/18	10/18	12/18	2/19	4/19
Oil Burning		4/21 to 9/21		6/21 - 8/21	
		6/26 to 12/26		6/26 - 12/26	
SR Livery, E prefix	7/24	10/25	5/24	10/24	7/24
Named	2/25	10/25	8/25	11/25	11/25
King Arthur Chimney	9/28	10/25	7/28	1/28	1/27
Smoke Deflectors	9/28	6/28	7/28	1/28	5/28
Maunsell Superheater	9/30	6/29	3/30	5/30	12/29
Maunsell Boiler (k)	1/37 to 4/40	12/25 to 4/30 (j)	6/34 to 8/35	12/35 to 1/38	2/35 to 9/37
	11/50 to 11/56	2/32 to 6/34	5/41 to 2/44		8/46 to 4/50 (p)
		7/40 to 10/42			4/50 to 12/55
E-Prefix removed	2/32	2/32	10/32	8/31	11/31
Bulleid Green (1)	12/38 (a)	4/39 (a)	4/39 (a)	7/40 (e)	11/39 (d)
Bulleid Green (2)	5/40 (d)	7/40 (e)	5/41 (g)		
Bulleid Black	7/42	11/42	3/44	8/42	10/42
Lemaître Exhaust	12/40	2/41			
Bulleid Green	7/47 (e)	10/46 (e)	3/47 (h)	2/49 (e)	8/46 (e)
Oil Burning					12/46 to 10/48
Electric Lighting					1/48
BR Number	2/49 (xs)	7/49 (xs)	5/49 (wse)	2/49 (ws)	10/48 (xs)
Snifting Valves removed	11/50	12/47	5/49	2/49	5/50
BR Dark Green	11/50	6/51	1/53	5/52	5/50
Totem	small	small	small		
Withdrawn	3/11/56	23/6/56	8/3/58	4/5/57	10/12/55
Recorded Mileage	1,455,334	1,412,683	1,460,218	1,399,989	1,357,971

Bulleid Green liveries applied between 1938 and 1942 also from 1946
(a) Maunsell Green, black edging, white lining, black smoke deflectors and tender coping
(d) Olive Green, black edging, yellow lining, green smoke deflectors and tender coping
(e) Malachite Green, black edging, yellow lining, green smoke deflectors and tender coping
(g) Malachite Green, unlined, smoke deflector colour not known, tender coping probably green
(h) Style (e) but lighter shade of Malachite Green used; returned to regular colour May 1949.

Bulleid Black livery
The dates shown are the next General (Class A) Overhaul date after June 1942.

British Railways number
(x) Renumbered in Bulleid numerals whilst retaining SOUTHERN lettering on tender
(w) Renumbered in Gill Sans numerals with no lettering on tender
(s) Smokebox number plate fitted
(j) Maunsell boiler, with Eastleigh superheater until June 1929
(k) Dates confirmed by Engine and Boiler Record Cards, there may have been others before 1935
(p) Maunsell boiler with 4+5 washout plugs

Urie 'Arthurs' - All built at Eastleigh Works

Number	741	742	743	744	745
Name	*Joyous Gard*	*Camelot*	*Lyonnesse*	*Maid of Astolat*	*Tintagel*
Works Order No	P.15-1	P.15-2	P.15-3	P.15-4	P.15-5
To Traffic	4/19	6/19	8/19	9/19	11/19
SR Livery, E prefix	1/24	1/24	6/25	10/24	9/24
Named	6/25	12/25	6/25	4/25	4/25
King Arthur Chimney	6/25	12/25 (h)	6/25	6/27	7/28
Smoke Deflectors	1/28	6/28	11/28	11/27	7/28
E-Prefix Removed	9/32	2/32	1/33	1/32	1/32
Maunsell Superheater	2/29	8/30	6/30	1/30	1/32
Maunsell Boiler (k)	9/32 to 9/34	6/28 to 3/32 (j)	6/36 to 2/37	2/34 to 10/35	6/49 to 7/51
	9/49 to 3/53	4/46 to 9/48	6/49 to 6/53 (p)	10/54 to 1/56 (p)	
			6/53 to 10/55		
Bulleid Green (1)	4/40 (d)	6/39 (d)	2/39 (a)	11/39 (d)	4/39 (c)
Bulleid Green (2)			5/41 (e)	3/42 (e)	6/41 (e)
Bulleid Black	11/42	6/42	8/44	7/45	6/44
Lemaître Exhaust	12/40				
Bulleid Green	8/46 (e)	8/46 (e)	12/46 (e)	6/48 (e)	11/46 (e)
Oil Burning					10/47 to 12/48
Electric Lighting					10/47
BR Number	11/48 (xs)	10/48 (zs)	6/49 (ws)	6/48 (y)	12/48 (xs)
Snifting Valves removed	3/48	10/48	6/49	6/48	10/47
BR Dark Green	9/49	12/51	6/53	4/51	8/51
Totem	small 4/53	small	small	small	small
Withdrawn	4/2/56	9/2/57	6/10/55	7/1/56	11/2/56
Recorded Mileage	1,346,891	1,386,007	1,301,442	1,463,292	1,464,032

Bulleid Green liveries applied between 1938 and 1942 and from 1946
(a) Maunsell Green, black edging, white lining, black smoke deflectors and tender coping
(c) Olive Green, Dark Green edging, yellow lining, green smoke deflectors
(d) Olive Green, black edging, yellow lining, green smoke deflectors and tender coping
(e) Malachite Green, black edging, yellow lining, green smoke deflectors and tender coping

Bulleid Black livery
The dates shown are the next General (Class A) overhaul date after June 1942.

British Railways number
(x) Renumbered in Bulleid numerals whilst retaining SOUTHERN lettering on tender
(y) Renumbered in Bulleid numerals with BRITISH RAILWAYS in Sunshine lettering
(z) Renumbered in Gill Sans numerals with BRITISH RAILWAYS in Gill Sans lettering
(w) Renumbered in Gill Sans numerals with no lettering on tender
(s) Smokebox number plate fitted
(h) No 742 carried a tall lipped chimney between July 1924 and December 1925
(j) Maunsell boiler with Eastleigh superheater
(k) Dates confirmed by Engine and Boiler Record Cards, there may have been others before 1935
(p) Maunsell boiler with 4+5 washout plugs

Urie 'Arthurs' - All built at Eastleigh Works

Number	746	747	748	749	750
Name	*Pendragon*	*Elaine*	*Vivien*	*Iseult*	*Morgan le Fay*
Works Order No	L.16-1	L.16-2	L.16-3	L.16-4	L.16-5
To Traffic	6/22	7/22	8/22	9/22	10/22
SR Livery, E prefix	12/24	1/25	4/25	4/24	4/24
Named	10/25	9/25	4/25	9/25	10/25
King Arthur Chimney	1/29	9/25 (h)	11/29	9/25	1/28
Smoke Deflectors (1)	1/29	8/28	11/29	8/27	1/28
Smoke Deflectors (2)					
Maunsell Superheater	1/29	11/30	11/29	12/28	2/30
Maunsell Boiler (k)	7/46 to 10/55 (p)		11/35 to 10/37 9/50 to 9/57	11/38 to 6/41	2/29 to 2/32 1/50 to 8/55
E-Prefix Removed	10/32	6/32	5/32	5/32	11/31
Bulleid Green (1)	3/39 (b)	2/40 (d)	11/38 (a)	7/40 (e)	4/41 (e)
Bulleid Green (2)	7/41 (e)		7/41 (e)	9/40 (f)	
Bulleid Black	1/44	7/42	5/45	9/42	11/43
Bulleid Green	7/46 (e)	1/48 (e)	9/47 (e)	3/47 (e)	2/48 (e)
Oil Burning			9/47 - 11/48	10/47 - 11/48	
Electric Light			12/47	11/47	
S-Prefix		1/48 (y)			2/48 (y)
BR Number	9/50 (s)	5/50 (s)	11/48 (xs)	11/48 (xs)	11/48 (y)
Snifting Valves removed	9/50	2/48	9/47	10/47	1/48
BR Dark Green	9/50	5/50	9/50	11/51	1/50
Totem	small	small	small	small	large/small
Withdrawn	22/10/55	20/10/56	7/9/57	19/6/57	6/7/57
Recorded Mileage	1,388,102	1,296,927	1,298,717	1,261,799	1,298,672

Bulleid Green liveries applied between 1938 and 1942 and from 1946
(a) Maunsell Green, black edging, white lining, black smoke deflectors and tender coping
(b) Malachite Green, black edging, white lining, black smoke deflectors and tender coping
(d) Olive Green, black edging, yellow lining, green smoke deflectors and tender coping
(e) Malachite Green, black edging, yellow lining, green smoke deflectors and tender coping
(f) Maunsell Green, green edging, yellow lining, smoke deflector and tender coping colour not known

British Railways number
(x) Renumbered in Bulleid numerals whilst retaining SOUTHERN lettering on tender
(y) Renumbered in Bulleid numerals with BRITISH RAILWAYS in Sunshine lettering
(z) Renumbered in Gill Sans numerals with BRITISH RAILWAYS in Gill Sans lettering
(s) Smokebox number plate fitted
(h) No 747 carried a Lord Nelson-pattern chimney between 30 November and 6 December 1937
(k) Dates confirmed by Engine and Boiler Record Cards, there may have been others before 1935
(p) Maunsell boiler with 4+5 washout plugs

Bulleid Black livery
The dates shown are the next General (Class A) overhaul date after June 1942.

Urie 'Arthurs' - All built at Eastleigh Works

Number	751	752	753	754	755
Name	*Etarre*	*Linette*	*Melisande*	*The Green Knight*	*The Red Knight*
Works Order No	N.16-1	N.16-2	N.16-3	N.16-4	N.16-5
SR Livery, E prefix	4/24	12/24	1/25	9/25	4/25
Named	3/27	3/27	8/25	9/25	4/25
King Arthur Chimney	12/28	12/28 (l)	5/26	9/25	7/27
Smoke Deflectors (1)	12/28	12/27	6/26 (i)	7/28	1/28
Smoke Deflectors (2)			1/28		
Maunsell Superheater	6/29	9/30	7/28	1/30	3/29
Maunsell Boiler (k)	12/35 to 12/36 1/55 to 6/57	1/37 to 2/39 11/50 to 12/55	9/31 to 9/33 4/37 to 6/39 10/42 to 1/46		
E-Prefix removed	10/31	3/32	9/31	6/32	2/32
Bulleid Green (1)	1/39 (a)	3/39 (a)	7/39 (d)	2/39 (a)	2/40 (d)
Bulleid Green (2)	5/41 (e)	2/41 (f)		10/41 (e)	
Bulleid Black	4/44	2/45	11/42	11/45	8/42
Lamaître Exhaust		2/41			2/40
Bulleid Green	6/48 (e)	3/47 (e)	4/48 (e)	1/48 (e)	4/46 (e)
Oil Burning		9/47 to 10/48			
Electric Lighting		12/47			
S-Prefix				1/48 (x)	
BR Number	6/48 (zs)	9/48 (zs)	4/48 (y)	7/48 (s)	10/49 (s)
Snifting Valves removed	6/48	11/50	3/48	1/48	10/49
BR Dark Green	4/51	11/50	9/50 (s)	4/50	10/49
Totem	small	small	small	small	large/small
Withdrawn	15/6/57	10/12/55	16/3/57	10/2/53	11/5/57
Recorded Mileage	1,361,472	1,287,576	1,241,374	1,151,285	1,330,274

Bulleid Green liveries applied between 1938 and 1942 and from 1946
(a) Maunsell Green, black edging, white lining, black smoke deflectors and tender coping
(d) Olive Green, black edging, yellow lining, green smoke deflectors and tender coping
(e) Malachite Green, black edging, yellow lining, green smoke deflectors and tender coping
(f) Maunsell Green, green edging, yellow lining, black smoke deflectors, tender coping colour not known
(g) Malachite Green, unlined, smoke deflector colour not known, tender coping probably green

British Railways number
(x) No 754 received an S-prefix in Bulleid numerals whilst retaining SOUTHERN lettering on tender. However, the S-prefix was removed before the locomotive went to traffic. Presumably, the cabside numerals were then offset, but there is no photographic proof.
(y) Renumbered in Bulleid numerals with BRITISH RAILWAYS in Sunshine lettering
(z) Renumbered in Gill Sans numerals with BRITISH RAILWAYS in Gill Sans lettering
(s) Smokebox number plate fitted
(i) No 753 had a curved deflector on top of the smokebox between 21 May 1926 and 16 June 1926
(k) Dates confirmed by Engine and Boiler Record Cards, there may have been others before 1935
(l) No 752 was the only Urie Arthur to run with smoke deflectors whilst fitted with a stovepipe chimney

Bulleid Black livery
The dates shown are the next shopping date after June 1942.

Eastleigh 'Arthurs' - All built at Eastleigh Works

Number	E448	E449	E450	E451	E452
Name	*Sir Tristram*	*Sir Torre*	*Sir Kay*	*Sir Lamorak*	*Sir Meliagrance*
Works Order No	C.17-1	C.17-2	C.17-3	C.17-4	C.17-5
To Traffic	5/25	6/25	6/25	6/25	7/25
Urie Tender		6/25 (i)			
Smoke Deflectors (1)	2/29	4/29	2/26 (j)	11/27	12/27
Smoke Deflectors (2)			12/27		
E-Prefix removed	5/33	5/33	6/32	5/32	10/31
Flaman Speed Recorder			1/39 -to12/40	10/27 to 7/30	
4+5 Washout Plug Boiler	5/39 to 8/43			12/38 to 10/40	
				4/45 to 12/47	
Bulleid Green (1)	6/39 (c)	4/39 (a)	6/39 (d)	1/39 (a)	5/39 (c)
Bulleid Green (2)	10/41 (e)	11/40 (b)	2/41 (e)	12/40 (e)	9/40 (e)
Bulleid Black	9/43	9/43	11/42	6/42	1/43
Bulleid Green	8/48 (e)	11/47 (e)	12/47 (e)	12/47 (e)	5/48 (e)
BR Number	8/48 (zst)	9/49 (s)	9/49 (s)	7/48 (xs)	5/48 (u)
Snifting Valves removed	10/47	9/49	12/47	12/47	5/48
BR Dark Green	12/51	9/49	9/49	2/50	5/52
First Totem	small	large/small	large/small	large/small	small
Urie Tender	5/55	11/55	10/56	1/57 (l)	6/57
Second Totem	none	none	10/58	1/61	none
Withdrawn	22/8/60	19/12/59	3/9/60	16/6/62	22/8/59
Recorded Mileage	1,483,140	1,373,426	1,478,783	1,579,556	1,494,011

Bulleid Green liveries applied between 1938 and 1942 then from 1946
(a) Maunsell Green, black edging, white lining, black smoke deflectors and tender coping
(b) Malachite Green, black edging, white lining, black smoke deflectors and tender coping
(c) Olive Green, Dark Green edging, yellow lining, green smoke deflectors
(d) Olive Green, black edging, yellow lining, green smoke deflectors and tender coping
(e) Malachite Green, black edging, yellow lining, green smoke deflectors and tender coping

Bulleid Black livery
The dates shown are the next General (Class A) overhaul date after June 1942.

British Railways number
(x) Renumbered in Bulleid numerals whilst retaining SOUTHERN lettering on tender
(z) Renumbered in Gill Sans numerals with BRITISH RAILWAYS in Gill Sans lettering
(w) Renumbered in Gill Sans numerals with no lettering on tender
(s) Smokebox number plate fitted
(t) No 30448 was numbered and lettered in Gill Sans, but with Bulleid numerals on rear of tender
(u) No 30452 Renumbered May 1948 in Bulleid numerals with BRITISH RAILWAYS in Gill Sans lettering then part repaint June 1950 with Gill Sans numerals and smokebox plate
(i) E449 was fitted with a Urie tender for the Stockton & Darlington Centenary, retained to at least September 1925
(j) E450 had small wing plated behind the chimney from February 1926 to March 1927
(l) Urie tender with steps and handrail at the rear from 'Remembrance' class locomotive, with steps and handrail at the rear

Left:
No 754 *The Green Knight* alongside class T9 No 302 at Eastleigh shed in 1937. (CR/SLS)

Eastleigh 'Arthurs' - All built at Eastleigh Works

Number	E453	E454	E455	E456	E457
Name	*King Arthur*	*Queen Guinevere*	*Sir Launcelot*	*Sir Galahad*	*Sir Bedivere*
Works Order No	B.17-1	B.17-2	B.17-3	B.17-4	B.17-5
To Traffic	2/25	3/25	3/25	4/25	4/25
Smoke Deflectors (1)	4/27 (j)	7/28	3/28	3/28	c. 1927 (k)
Smoke Deflectors (2)	7/28				2/28
E-Prefix removed	7/31	8/32	3/32	7/31	8/32
Flaman Speed Recorder					8/38 to c. 1941
4+5 Washout Plug Boiler		10/35 to 2/37	8/37 to 4/39	11/55 to 6/58	12/59 to 5/61
Bulleid Green (1)	7/39 (d)	1/40 (d)	5/39 (d)	6/40 (d)	7/39 (d)
Bulleid Green (2)	3/41 (e)	1/42 (e)	11/41 (e)		6/41 (e)
Bulleid Black	11/42	2/44	10/42	4/42	5/43
Bulleid Green	9/47 (e)	3/49 (e)	5/48 (e)	12/46 (e)	1/47 (e)
S-Prefix	1/48 (y)				
BR Number	2/50 (s)	3/49 (ws)	5/48 (y)	10/48 (zs)	8/49 (s)
Snifting Valves removed	2/48	3/49	5/48	10/48	8/49
BR Dark Green	2/50	4/51	5/50	3/52	8/49
First Totem	large/small	small	small	small	
Urie Tender	4/57	6/57	12/57	8/58	6/55 (l)
Second Totem	4/57 (m)				2/59
Withdrawn	8/7/61	18/10/58	18/4/59	14/5/60	20/5/61
Recorded Mileage	1,606,428	1,421,676	1,475,829	1,386,742	1,429,723

Bulleid Green liveries applied between 1938 and 1942 then from 1946
(d) Olive Green, black edging, yellow lining, green smoke deflectors and tender coping
(e) Malachite Green, black edging, yellow lining, green smoke deflectors and tender coping

Bulleid Black livery
The dates shown are the next General (Class A) overhaul date after June 1942.

British Railways number
(y) Renumbered in Bulleid numerals with BRITISH RAILWAYS in Sunshine lettering
(z) Renumbered in Gill Sans numerals with BRITISH RAILWAYS in Gill Sans lettering
(w) Renumbered in Gill Sans numerals with no lettering on tender
(s) Smokebox number plate fitted
(j) E453 had short deflector plates from April 1927 to July 1928
(k) E457 ran circa 1927 with a curved shield at rear of chimney
(l) 5200-gallon tender from Urie 'H15', 6in deeper and 4in narrower than standard Urie 5,000-gallon tender
(m) No 30453 received a Urie tender with a small second totem in March 1957, repainted with large totem in July 1958

Scotch 'Arthurs' - All built by North British Locomotive Company

Number	E763	E764	E765	E766	E767
Name	*Sir Bors de Ganis*	*Sir Gawain*	*Sir Gareth*	*Sir Geraint*	*Sir Valence*
Works No	23209	23210	23211	23212	23213
To Traffic	5/25	5/25	5/25	5/25	5/25
Smoke Deflectors	6/28	4/28	11/27	2/28	4/28
E-Prefix R removed	4/32	8/32	4/33	7/31	9/31
4000 gal 6-wheel Tender	6/28	4/28	1/29	1/29	2/30
5,000 gal Urie Tender	10/36 (t)	11/36	12/36	7/37	6/37
Flaman Speed Recorder					8/38 to c. 1941
4+5 Washout Plug Boiler				6/53 to 12/58	
Bulleid Green (1)	10/41 (e)	1/39 (a)	7/40 (e)	3/39 (b)	1/41 (e)
Bulleid Green (2)		1/42 (e)		5/41 (e)	
Bulleid Black	2/43	1/44	2/43	3/44	7/43
Bulleid Green	9/47 (e)	2/49 (e)	3/49 (e)	4/46 (e)	3/46 (e)
BR Number	6/50(s)	2/49 (ws)	3/49 (ws)	1/49 (ws)	11/48 (zs)
Snifting Valves removed	9/47	2/49	3/49	11/47	11/48
BR Dark Green	6/50	3/52	2/52	3/51	10/51
First Totem	small	small	small	small	small
Second Totem	6/58	none	4/60	none	none
Withdrawn	1/10/60	22/7/61	29/9/62	27/12/58	27/6/59
Recorded Mileage	1,050,454	979,213	1,116,054	1,141,019	1,029,937

Bulleid Green liveries applied between 1938 and 1942 then from 1946
(a) Maunsell Green, black edging, white lining, black smoke deflectors and tender coping
(b) Malachite Green, black edging, white lining, black smoke deflectors and tender coping
(e) Malachite Green, black edging, yellow lining, green smoke deflectors and tender coping

Bulleid Black livery
The dates shown are the next General (Class A) overhaul date after June 1942.

British Railways number
(z) Renumbered in Gill Sans numerals with BRITISH RAILWAYS in Gill Sans lettering
(w) Renumbered in Gill Sans numerals with no lettering on tender
(s) Smokebox number plate fitted
(t) No 30763 fitted with a tender with modified footsteps from a 'Remembrance' class locomotive in March 1956

Scotch 'Arthurs' - All built by North British Locomotive Company

Number	E768	E769	E770 (nrc)	E771	E772
Name	*Sir Balin*	*Sir Balan*	*Sir Prianius*	*Sir Sagramore*	*Sir Percivale*
Works No	23214	23215	23216	23217	23218
To Traffic	5/25	6/25	6/25	6/25	6/25
Smoke Deflectors (1)	6/28	3/28	3/28	10/28	9/26 (j)
Smoke Deflectors (2)					10/32
E-Prefix removed	3/32	7/31	7/32	4/32	10/32
4000 gal 6-wheel Tender	6/28	none	12/28	10/28	11/28
5,000 gal flat side Tender	1/30	12/29	5/30	5/30	7/30
5,000 gal Urie Tender	3/32 (k)	7/31 (k)	7/32 (k)	7/32 (k)	6/32 (k)
Bulleid Green	6/40 (d)	7/40 (e)	6/39 (d)	none	2/40 (d)
Bulleid Black	9/43	11/44	1/43	7/42	3/43
Bulleid Green	9/47 (e)	5/47 (e)	11/47 (e)	5/47 (e)	7/47 (e)
BR Number	10/48 (zs)	4/51 (s)	7/51 (s)	5/50 (s)	4/48 (y)
Snifting Valves removed	10/48	4/51	11/47	5/50	7/47
BR Dark Green	6/52	4/51	7/51	5/50	12/49
First Totem	small	small	small	small	large/small
Second Totem	2/58	none	8/57	6/57	none
Withdrawn	4/11/61	27/3/60	24/11/62	23/2/61	30/9/61
Recorded Mileage	1,078,112	1,036,794	1,144,608	1,054,549	1,187,768

Bulleid Green liveries applied between 1938 and 1942 then from 1946
(d) Olive Green, black edging, yellow lining, green smoke deflectors and tender coping
(e) Malachite Green, black edging, yellow lining, green smoke deflectors and tender coping

Bulleid Black livery
The dates shown are the next General (Class A) overhaul date after June 1942.

British Railways number
(y) Renumbered in Bulleid numerals with BRITISH RAILWAYS in Sunshine lettering
(z) Renumbered in Gill Sans numerals with BRITISH RAILWAYS in Gill Sans lettering
(s) Smokebox number plate fitted
(j) E772 had large deflector plates from September 1929 to October 1932
(k) Urie tenders with three vacuum reservoirs bvehind the coal space from LN class locomotives.
(nrc) E 770, No Record Card held by NRM Library in York, some data not available

Scotch 'Arthurs' - All built by North British Locomotive Company

Number	E773	E774	E775	E776	E777
Name	*Sir Lavaine*	*Sir Gaheris*	*Sir Agravaine*	*Sir Galagars*	*Sir Lamiel*
Works No	23219	23220	23221	23222	23223
To Traffic	7/25	6/25	6/25	6/25	6/25
Smoke Deflectors (1)	12/27	(n)	12/27	12/27	12/27
Smoke Deflectors (2)	(m)	6/27			
E-Prefix Removed	11/32	10/32	10/31	6/32	6/32
4+5 Washout Plug Boiler	10/47 to 4/49	3/49 to 9/55			5/42 to 12/46
	1/60 to 2/62				
Bulleid Green (1)	5/40 (d)	12/39 (d)	5/39 (c)	2/39 (a)	10/39 (d)
Bulleid Green (2)			7/41 (e)	12/40 (e)	
Bulleid Black	4/43	8/42	11/43	8/42	7/44
Bulleid Green	11/47 (e)	11/46 (e)	10/46 (e)	3/46 (e)	1/47 (e)
BR Number	6/48 (xs)	4/49 (ws)	11/49 (s)	7/49 (s)	5/48 (xv)
Snifting Valves removed	11/47	4/49	11/49	12/47	10/48
BR Dark Green	9/51	5/52	11/49	6/50	12/51
First Totem	small	small	large/small	small	small
Second Totem	1/60	none	none	10/57	1/60
Withdrawn	10/2/62	9/1/60	27/2/60	24/1/59	21/10/61
Recorded Mileage	1,296,365	1,121,270	1,136,498	1,094,727	1,257,638

Bulleid Green liveries applied between 1938 and 1942 then from 1946
(a) Maunsell Green, black edging, white lining, black smoke deflectors and tender coping
(c) Olive Green, Dark Green edging, yellow lining, green smoke deflectors
(d) Olive Green, black edging, yellow lining, green smoke deflectors and tender coping
(e) Malachite Green, black edging, yellow lining, green smoke deflectors and tender coping

Bulleid Black Livery
The dates shown are the next General (Class A) overhaul date after June 1942.

British Railways number
(x) Renumbered in Bulleid numerals whilst retaining SOUTHERN lettering on tender
(w) Renumbered in Gill Sans numerals with no tender lettering, black wheels and smoke deflectors
(v) No 30777 was repainted in Malachite Green with Gill Sans lettering and smokebox plate in October 1948
(s) Smokebox number plate fitted
(m) E773 had a circular projection in front of the smokebox for a time circa 1930, then returned to standard
(n) E774 had a curved strip on the front of the smokebox, as on No 753

Scotch 'Arthurs' - All built by North British Locomotive Company

Number	E778 (nrc)	E779	E780	E781	E782
Name	*Sir Pelleas*	*Sir Colgrevance*	*Sir Persant*	*Sir Aglovale*	*Sir Brian*
Works No	23224	23225	23226	23227	23228
To Traffic	7/25	7/25	7/25	8/25	7/25
Smoke Deflectors	1/28	4/27 (o)	12/27	12/27	12/27
E-Prefix Removed	8/31	1/32	7/32	1/33	7/31
Flaman Speed Recorder		8/38 to c.1941			10/27 to 12/30
4+5 Washout Plug Boiler		6/42 to 4/44			9/49 to 1/50
		3/47 to 9/48			
Bulleid Green (1)	11/39 (d)	8/40 (e)	2/40 (d)	11/39 (d)	2/39 (a)
Bulleid Green (2)				1/42 (e)	10/41 (e)
Bulleid Black	2/43	8/42	11/42	2/43	8/44
Bulleid Green	11/46 (e)	4/47 (e)	3/47 (eh)	10/47 (e)	none
BR Number	11/49 (s)	10/48 (xs)	1/50 (s)	3/49 (xs)	5/48 (v)
Snifting Valves removed	11/49	10/48	1/50	10/47	10/49
BR Dark Green	11/49	10/49	1/50	5/51	10/49 (s)
First Totem	large/small	large/small	large/small	small	large/small
Second Totem	none	5/57	none	11/57	5/60
Withdrawn	23/5/59	11/7/59	11/7/59	12/5/62	15/9/62
Recorded Mileage	1,174,925	1,305,864	1,112,973	1,184,126	1,197,719

Bulleid Green liveries applied between 1938 and 1942 then from 1946
(a) Maunsell Green, black edging, white lining, black smoke deflectors and tender coping
(d) Olive Green, black edging, yellow lining, green smoke deflectors and tender coping
(e) Malachite Green, black edging, yellow lining, green smoke deflectors and tender coping
(h) Lighter shade of Malachite Green used, returned to regular colour May 1949.

Bulleid Black livery
The dates shown are the next General (Class A) overhaul date after June 1942.

British Railways number
(x) Renumbered in Bulleid numerals whilst retaining SOUTHERN lettering on tender
(v) No 30782 received the BR number on black Southern livery
(s) Smokebox number plate fitted
(o) E779 was the first locomotive with 'standard' smoke deflectors; no cut out for the steam pipe cladding.
(nrc) E 778, No Record Card held by NRM Library in York, some data not available

Scotch 'Arthurs' - All built by North British Locomotive Company

Number	E783	E784	E785	E786	E787
Name	*Sir Gillemere*	*Sir Nerovens*	*Sir Mador de la Porte*	*Sir Lionel*	*Sir Menadeuke*
Works No	23279	23280	23281	23282	23283
To Traffic	8/25	8/25	9/25	9/25	9/25
Smoke Deflectors (1)	3/27 (p)	1/28	2/28	2/30	11/27
Smoke Deflectors (2)	12/27				
E-Prefix removed	2/32	12/31	2/32	4/32	8/31
4+5 Washout Plug Boiler	4/43 to 6/46	11/38 to 11/40	9/35 to 6/36 10/44 - 6/47	11/39 to 9/42	
Bulleid Green (1)	11/40 (e)	12/38 (a)	12/38 (a)	12/39 (d)	2/39 (a)
Bulleid Green (2)		1/41 (e)	7/40 (e)		11/40 (e)
Multiple Chimneys	1940 to 41				
Bulleid Black	5/43	6/43	8/43	10/42	8/43
Bulleid Green	7/46 (e)	5/48 (e)	6/47 (e)	10/47 (e)	3/48
S-Prefix					3/48 (y)
BR Number	5/48 (x)	5/48 (y)	8/48 (xs)	10/48 (xsw)	4/49 (s)
Snifting Valves removed	5/48	5/48	2/49	10/47	3/48
Spark Arrester		6/47 to 5/48 2/49 to 10/54			
BR Dark Green	7/49	11/50	6/51	12/52	11/50
First Totem	small	small		small	small
Second Totem				12/57	
Withdrawn	4/3/61	17/10/59	17/10/59	29/8/59	28/2/59
Recorded Mileage	1,221,647	1,369,983	1,314,287	1,389,822	1,304,180

Bulleid Green liveries applied between 1938 and 1942 then from 1946
(a) Maunsell Green, black edging, white lining, black smoke deflectors and tender coping
(d) Olive Green, black edging, yellow lining, green smoke deflectors and tender coping
(e) Malachite Green, black edging, yellow lining, green smoke deflectors and tender coping

Bulleid Black livery
The dates shown are the next General (Class A) overhaul date after June 1942.

British Railways number
(x) Renumbered in Bulleid numerals whilst retaining SOUTHERN lettering on tender
(y) Renumbered in Bulleid numerals with BRITISH RAILWAYS in Sunshine lettering
(w) No 30786 repainted with Gill Sans numerals, blank tender, black wheels and smoke deflectors July 1949
(s) Smokebox number plate fitted
(p) E783 had a shovel-shaped device in front of the chimney from March 1927 to December 1927

Scotch 'Arthurs' - All built by North British Locomotive Company

Number	E788	E789	E790	E791	E792
Name	*Sir Urre of the Mount*	*Sir Guy*	*Sir Villiars*	*Sir Uwaine*	*Sir Hervis de Revel*
Works No	23284	23285	23286	23287	23288
To Traffic	9/25	9/25	9/25	9/25	9/25
Smoke Deflectors	12/27 (p)	8/28	2/28	1/28	4/28
E-Prefix removed	1/32	1/32	1/32	12/31	1/32
4+5 Washout Plug Boiler			3/47 to 10/48		
Lemaître Exhaust					9/40 to 3/52
Bulleid Green (1)	9/39 (d)	3/39 (b)	4/39 (c)	8/40 (e)	9/40 (e)
Bulleid Green (2)	12/41 (e)	1/41 (e)	3/41 (e)		
Bulleid Black	1/43	5/43	1/43	9/42	1/43
Bulleid Green	10/46 (e)	3/46 (e)	9/46 (e)	12/48 (e)	5/47 (e)
Spark Arrester	12/49 to 6/51				
BR Number	10/48 (zs)	9/48 (zs)	9/48 (zs)	12/48 (zs)	3/50 (s)
Snifting Valves removed	10/48	9/48	9/48	12/48	3/50
BR Dark Green	6/51	5/52	10/52	5/51	3/50
First Totem	small	small	small	small	large/small
Second Totem	3/60	none	5/57	6/57	none
Withdrawn	2/62	26/12/59	4/11/61	21/5/60	14/2/59
Recorded Mileage	1,423,378	1,383,297	1,404,162	1,353,546	1,351,319

Bulleid Green liveries applied between 1938 and 1942 then from 1946
(b) Light Malachite Green, black edging, white lining, black smoke deflectors and tender coping
(c) Olive Green, Dark Green edging, yellow lining, green smoke deflectors
(d) Olive Green, black edging, yellow lining, green smoke deflectors and tender coping
(e) Malachite Green, black edging, yellow lining, green smoke deflectors and tender coping

Bulleid Black livery
The dates shown are the next General (Class A) overhaul date after June 1942.

British Railways number
(z) Renumbered in Gill Sans numerals with BRITISH RAILWAYS in Gill Sans lettering
(s) Smokebox number plate fitted

Second Series Eastleigh 'Arthurs' - All built at Eastleigh Works

Number	E793	E794	E795	E796	E797
Name	Sir Ontzlake	Sir Ector de Maris	Sir Dinadan	Sir Dodinas le Savage	Sir Blamor de Ganis
Works Order No	E121	E121	E121	E121	E121
To Traffic	3/26	3/26	4/26	4/26	6/26
Smoke Deflectors	4/29	5/28	1/30	2/31	1/29
E-Prefix removed	12/32	7/32	1/32	7/31	7/32
Flaman Speed Recorder	6/39 to c. 1941				
4+5 Washout Plug Boiler		4/55 to 9/58		6/53 to 10/57	
Bulleid Green	6/39 (d)	9/41 (e)	12/39 (d)	3/41 (e)	4/41 (e)
Bulleid Black	12/42	5/44	11/43	5/44	9/45
Bulleid Green	4/46 (e)	9/47 (e)	6/46 (e)	12/46 (e)	10/47 (e)
BR Number	10/48 (zs)	1/49 (xs)	3/49 (ws)	2/50 (s)	1/49 (ws)
Snifting Valves removed	10/48	9/47	3/49	2/50	10/47
BR Dark Green	5/51	6/50	9/52	2/50	10/51
First Totem	small	small	small	large/small	small
Second Totem	8/57	none	none	11/57	none
Urie Tender	9/59	none	3/58	1/61	none
Second Totem	9/59	none	5/58	1/61	none
Withdrawn	1/9/62	20/8/60	4/8/62	2/3/62	30/5/59
Recorded Mileage	979,964	903,663	963,712	1,061,295	953,718

Bulleid Green liveries applied between 1938 and 1942 then from 1946
(d) Olive Green, black edging, yellow lining, green smoke deflectors
(e) Malachite Green, black edging, yellow lining, green smoke deflectors

Bulleid Black livery
The dates shown are the next General (Class A) overhaul date after June 1942.

British Railways number
(x) Renumbered in Bulleid numerals whilst retaining SOUTHERN lettering on tender
(z) Renumbered in Gill Sans numerals with BRITISH RAILWAYS in Gill Sans lettering
(w) Renumbered in Gill Sans numerals with no lettering on tender
(s) Smokebox number plate fitted

Second Series Eastleigh 'Arthurs' - All built at Eastleigh Works

Number	E798	E799	E800	E801	E802
Name	Sir Hectimere	Sir Ironside	Sir Meleaus de Lile	Sir Meliot de Logres	Sir Durnore
Works Order No	E121	E121	E121	E121	E121
To Traffic	6/26	7/26	9/26	10/26	10/26
Smoke Deflectors	11/27	7/30	11/27	2/28	9/28
E-Prefix removed	2/33	5/32	11/32	10/32	10/31
Urie Boiler		11/34 to 8/37			
4+5 Washout Plug Boiler	1/31 to 7/37	9/43 to 12/46	11/35 to 4/37		5/41 to 10/44
Bulleid Green (1)	8/40 (e)	12/39 (d)	7/39 (d)	6/40 (e)	3/39 (a)
Bulleid Green (2)					11/41 (e)
Bulleid Black	4/45	10/43	2/45	11/43	12/44
Bulleid Green	11/47 (e)	1/47 (e)	none	10/46 (e)	12/46 (e)
BR Number	11/49 (s)	5/48 (ys)	11/49 (s)	7/49 (ws)	7/48 (zs)
Snifting Valves removed	11/47	3/49	11/49	7/49	7/48
BR Dark Green	11/49	6/50	11/49	3/51	1/51
First Totem	large/small	small	large/small	small	small
Urie Tender	11/60	none	1/59	none	6/58
Second Totem	11/60	none	1/59	none	6/58
Withdrawn	16/6/62	25/2/61	2/9/61	11/4/59	8/7/61
Recorded Mileage	1,093,868	1,001,005	960,510	939,617	1,096,024

Bulleid Green liveries applied between 1938 and 1942 then from 1946
(a) Maunsell Green, black edging, white lining, black smoke deflectors
(d) Olive Green, black edging, yellow lining, green smoke deflectors
(e) Malachite Green, black edging, yellow lining, green smoke deflectors

Bulleid Black livery
The dates shown are the next General (Class A) overhaul date after June 1942.

British Railways number
(y) Renumbered in Bulleid numerals with BRITISH RAILWAYS in Sunshine lettering
(z) Renumbered in Gill Sans numerals with BRITISH RAILWAYS in Gill Sans lettering
(w) Renumbered in Gill Sans numerals with no lettering on tender, black wheels and smoke deflectors
(s) Smokebox number plate fitted

cont. p.96 ▶

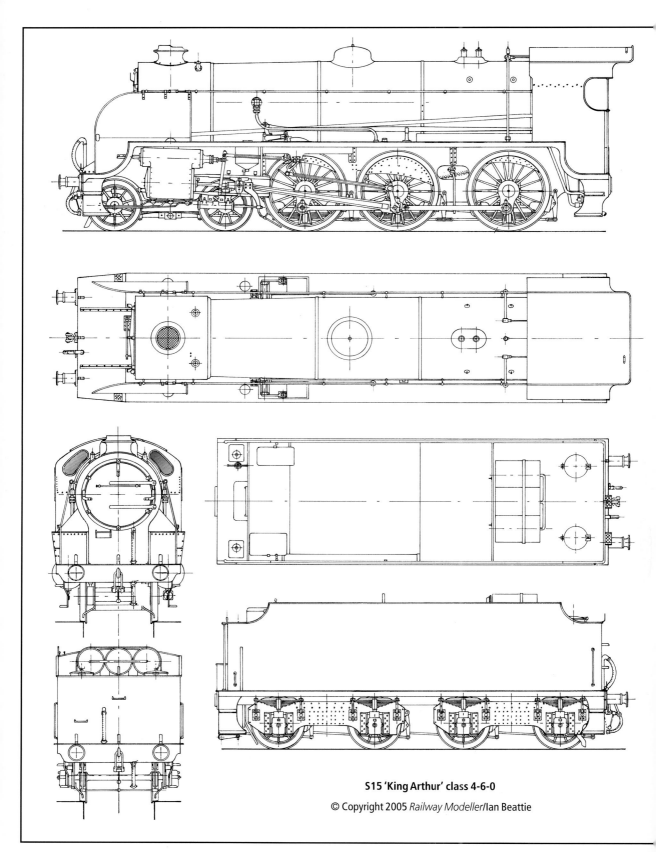

S15 'King Arthur' class 4-6-0

© Copyright 2005 *Railway Modeller*/Ian Beattie

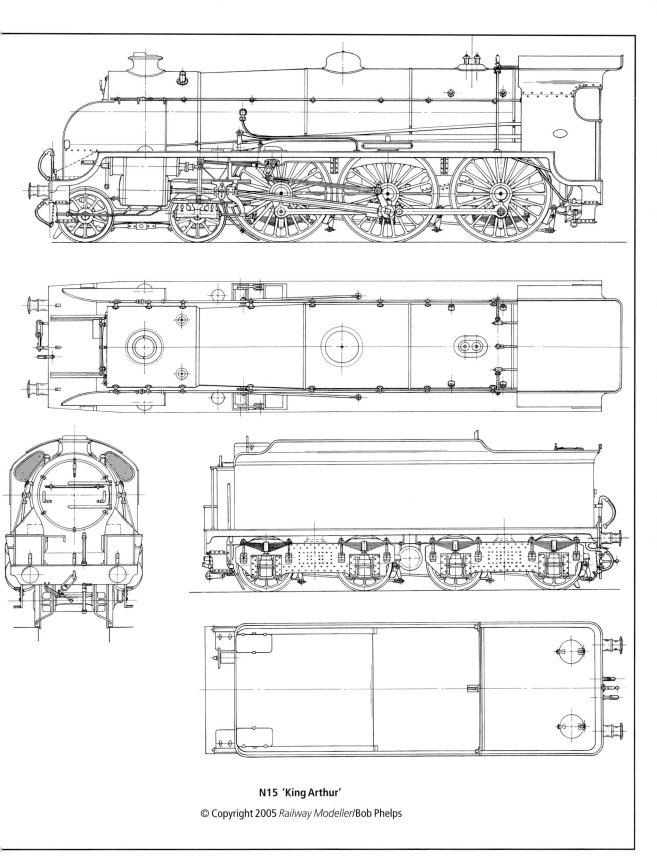

N15 'King Arthur'

4,000-gallon Tender (Drummond), as built

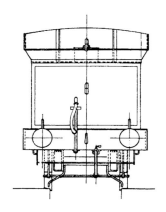
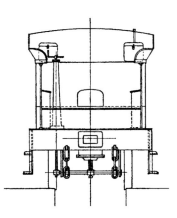

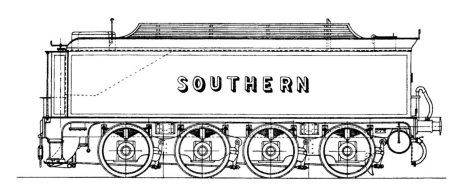

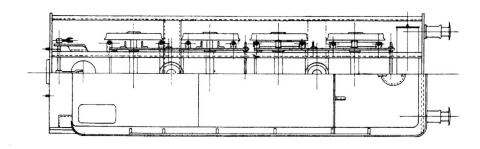

3,500-gallon Tender, for 'N15'

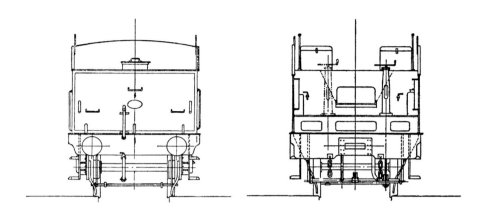

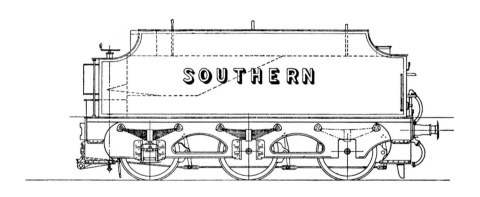

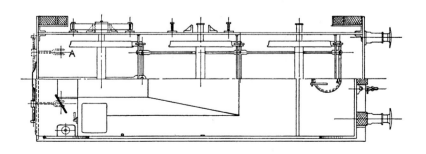

Second Series Eastleigh Arthurs - All built at Eastleigh Works

Number	E803	E804	E805	E806
Name	Sir Harry le Fise Lake	Sir Cador of Cornwall	Sir Constantine	Sir Galleron
Works Order No	E121	E121	E121	E121
To Traffic	11/26	12/26	1/27	1/27
Smoke Deflectors	3/28	10/28	12/28	4/28
E-Prefix removed	6/32	6/32	2/33	2/33
4+5 Washout Plug Boiler	6/48 to 5/50	5/45 to 1/50	12/35 to 6/39	
Bulleid Green (1)	10/39 (b)	2/42 (e)	7/39 (b)	5/40 (b)
Bulleid Green (2)			3/42 (e)	
Bulleid Black	9/42	7/45	10/44	11/43
Bulleid Green	2/47	5/47	10/48	5/47
BR Number	7/48 (zs)	11/48 (xs)	10/48 (zs)	9/48 (zs)
Snifting Valves Removed	7/48	5/47	10/48	9/48
BR Dark Green	12/51	2/50	12/51	11/50
First Totem	small	large/small	small	small
Urie Tender	11/59	none	none	9/58 (l)
Second Totem	none	4/57	6/57	9/58
Withdrawn	2/9/61	17/2/62	28/11/59	29/4/61
Recorded Mileage	989,396	1,115,634	1,019,198	1,127,096

Bulleid Green liveries applied between 1938 and 1942 then from 1946
(b) Malachite Green, black edging, white lining, black smoke deflectors
(e) Malachite Green, black edging, yellow lining, green smoke deflectors

Bulleid Black livery
Black was used for repaints between June 1942 and April 1946. The dates shown are the next shopping date after June 1942.

British Railways number
(x) Renumbered in Bulleid numerals whilst retaining SOUTHERN lettering on tender
(z) Renumbered in Gill Sans numerals with BRITISH RAILWAYS in Gill Sans lettering
(s) Smokebox number plate fitted
(l) Urie tender with curved steps and handrails on rear from 'Remembrance' class locoomotive

Above: The preserved No 777 *Sir Lamiel* crossing the Victoria Bridge over the River Severn. (AC)